THE SPY'S BEDSIDE BOOK

THE NEW BRITISH ARMY AEROPLANE

ROUGH SKETCH DRAWN BY LIEUT. KARL STRAUS

OF THE GERMAN SECRET SERVICE

THE SPY'S BEDSIDE BOOK

Graham Greene & Hugh Greene

That night I slept but little
WILLIAM LE QUEUX

CARROLL & GRAF PUBLISHERS, INC.
New York

First Carroll & Graf edition 1985

Carroll & Graf Publishers, Inc.
260 Fifth Avenue
New York, NY 10001

ISBN: 0-88184-188-9

Manufactured in the United States of America

TO THE IMMORTAL MEMORY

OF

WILLIAM LE QUEUX

AND

JOHN BUCHAN

THE trade of a spy is a very fine one, when the spy is working on his own account. Is it not in fact enjoying the excitements of a thief, while still retaining the character of an honest citizen? But a man who undertakes this trade must make up his mind to simmer with wrath, to fret with impatience, to stand about in the mud with his feet freezing, to be chilled or to be scorched, and to be deceived by false hopes. He must be ready, on the faith of a mere indication, to work up to an unknown goal; he must bear the disappointment of failing in his aim; he must be prepared to run, to be motionless, to remain for hours watching a window; to invent a thousand theories of action. . . . The only excitement which can compare with it is that of the life of a gambler.

HONORÉ DE BALZAC

Contents

INTRODUCTION. *Graham Greene*   *page* 11

FOR BEGINNERS

A Mission Is Proposed. *John Buchan*   17
Directive to Colonel Zabotin   27
A Damned Good Story. *W. Somerset Maugham*   28
A Late Call at the Germany Embassy. *L. C. Moyzisch*   30
The Value of Hide-and-seek. *Sir Robert Baden-Powell*   33
Take a Hard-boiled Egg. *Bernard Newman*   34
Example of Invisible Writing   35

HAZARDS OF THE PROFESSION

Tricked. *William Le Queux*   39
A Whip of the Circassian Sort. *T. E. Lawrence*   39
A Nasty Scratch. *William Le Queux*   40
A Spy Advertises. *Herbert Greene*   41
A Bathroom at the Paris Ritz. *Dennis Wheatley*   42
A Trussed Fowl. *William Le Queux*   43
In the Back of the Head. *Vladimir Petrov*   44
A Little Black Beret. *Peter Fleming*   46
At the Social Club. *George Griffith*   47
"That indeed is to die." *Fenimore Cooper*   52
Seduced with the Old Tricks. *W. H. Auden*   53
An Excellent Babadagly. *William Le Queux*   54
I Spy. *Graham Greene*   55
A Segment of German Sausage. *Peter Fleming*   59
The Sad Fate of Major André. *Richard Garnett and
    Anna Seward*   61

7

8 CONTENTS

The Police Spy. *Joseph Conrad* 65
Seven Miles from Calais. *Max Pemberton* 69
A Twinge. *William Le Queux* 75

DELIGHTS OF THE PROFESSION

A Narrow Squeak. *Sir Paul Dukes* 79
A Cross-country Run. *Belle Boyd* 82
Good Hunting. *Maurice Paléologue* 86
Foreign Travel. *Ian Fleming and Walter Schellenberg* 87
Seex Fat English Pigs. *Lechmere Worrall and J. E. Harold Terry* 88

ROOM AT THE BOTTOM

The Case of the Dixon Torpedo. *Arthur Morrison* 93
The Adventures of Bonaparte. *Compton Mackenzie* 115

UNEXPECTED ENCOUNTERS

Colette and Mata Hari. *Colette* 123
The Man in the Soft Cap. *Edmund Blunden* 125
A Meet in the Shires. *William Le Queux* 126

NOT KNOWN TO THE SECRET SERVICES

The Spies' March, 1913. *Rudyard Kipling* 131
A Royal Spy. *Alan H. Burgoyne* 134
Schnitzel alias Jones. *Richard Harding Davis* 139
How it Strikes a Contemporary. *Robert Browning* 161

SOME SIMPLE DISGUISES

Could Not Believe His Eyes. *Sir Robert Baden-Powell* 167
None Other Than . . . *William Le Queux* 168
The Waiters' Union. *E. Phillips Oppenheim* 168

PROFESSIONAL PERQUISITES

Royal Gifts. *William Le Queux* 181
A Well-appointed Office. *Walter Schellenberg* 181
Blanc de Blanc Brut, 1943. *Ian Fleming* 182
A Certificate from General Washington. *Fenimore Cooper* 184

SPARE-TIME ACTIVITIES

Prison Reading. *R. H. Bruce Lockhart* 193
Planning a Novel. *Eric Ambler* 193
Love. *Major André* 195

A GAGGLE OF SUSPECTS

Queer People. *Sir Basil Thomson* 199
The Lawrences. *Hugh Kingsmill* 203
Operation Goethe. *Thomas Mann* 205
What the Soldier Said. *William Blake* 205
Coleridge and Wordsworth, Suspects. *S. T. Coleridge* 206
The Gendarme and the Painter. *Paul Gauguin* 209
A Lawyer from Kent. *Walter Schellenberg* 210
The Amorous Duchess. *Maurice Paléologue* 210
Postscript to Dreyfus. *Guy Chapman* 212

TRICKS OF THE TRADE

Beneath the Open Windows. *Thomas Hardy* 215
The Ordinary Route. *Maurice Paléologue* 217
Equipment for Tibet. *Lieutenant-Colonel F. M. Bailey* 218
Vodka with Pepper. *Ian Fleming* 219
Dichlorethyl Sulphide. *R. L. Green* 219
Butterfly-hunting in Dalmatia. *Sir Robert Baden-Powell* 220

Carrier Pigeons. *H. R. Berndorff*   223
A Visit to the Lavatory. *R. H. Bruce Lockhart*   224
Top People Read "The Times". *William Le Queux*   225
The Ambassador's Valet. *Maurice Paléologue*   226
Russian Methods. *H. R. Berndorff*   228
The Explosive Cigar. *William Le Queux*   229
A Plant. *Admiral Sir William James*   230
The German Governess. The Simplest Thing in the
    World. An Early Microphone. *Lechmere Worrall
    and J. E. Harold Terry*   235
The Hansom Cab Approach. *George Griffith*   238
Calloway's Code. *O. Henry*   238

EPILOGUE. *Hugh Greene*   249

BIBLIOGRAPHY   253

Acknowledgments

FOR permission to reprint copyright passages the editors
and publisher wish to express their gratitude to all the living
authors concerned, and to Mrs George Bambridge, the Boy
Scouts Association, Jonathan Cape Ltd, Cassell and Co. Ltd,
Chatto and Windus Ltd, The Clarendon Press, Curtis
Brown Ltd, J. M. Dent and Sons Ltd, André Deutsch Ltd,
Doubleday and Co. Inc., Gerald Duckworth and Co. Ltd,
Faber and Faber Ltd, Samuel French Ltd, Robert Hale Ltd,
William Heinemann Ltd, Hodder and Stoughton Ltd, the
Hutchinson Group, Macmillan and Co. Ltd, Methuen and
Co. Ltd, the Arthur Morrison Executors, Max Parrish and
Co. Ltd, A. D. Peters, Putnam and Co. Ltd, Martin Secker
and Warburg Ltd, the Trustees of the Thomas Hardy Estate,
the Tweedsmuir Trustees, Ward, Lock and Co. Ltd, A. P.
Watt and Son, and Allan Wingate.

Introduction

I AM scarcely qualified to write this preface, for I doubt whether I have known more than a dozen spies in my life, and I am still uncertain about two of them—a certain Swiss business man whose notebook I borrowed for a few hours many years ago (strangely it contained the address of a friend of mine two thousand miles away who died a year later in a Nazi concentration camp), and another man of rather indeterminate origin with whom I planned to spend a Christmas holiday in the Banana Islands, in the company of two African blind dates—malaria robbed me of that holiday, somebody else's malaria, which made it worse. Of one spy, however, I have reason to be certain: he had hardly the qualifications of the others, for he was illiterate, he couldn't count above ten, and the only point of the compass he knew was the East, because he was a Mohammedan. I was reminded of him in recent years by the report of a divorce case in which the judge expressed severe criticisms of a private detective. The detective was also illiterate, he rode to his work on a bicycle and dictated his reports to his landlady who was stone deaf. Life is strange.

How very strange life is the readers of this anthology will certainly learn if they have not learned the lesson already. I wonder how many would be able to detect truth from fiction in this anthology if the editors had not printed the names of the contributors. Does Cicero's visit to the German Embassy in Ankara seem more or less fictional than Hannay's to the headquarters of the British Secret Service? Could the reader really tell which was fiction, between Mr Dennis Wheatley's

spy trapped in a bathroom at the Ritz, and Colonel Lawrence's
misadventure in Arabia? Of the two I find Mr Wheatley's
style a shade more convincing, for I cannot help wondering
how Lawrence, bent by his captors over a bench, could observe on his own body the marks of the Circassian whip. A
good spy should not embroider—it is Colonel Lawrence's
apparent embroidery which makes me, unwilling as I am to
side with Mr Aldington under any circumstances, distrust the
texture of his report. For in this strange funny nightmare
world we welcome the prosaic. An intimate friend of mine
once received simultaneously from two spies a report on the
contents of a concrete shed on an African airfield—one spy
said that it sheltered a tank, the other old boots. How could
my friend help being biased in favour of the old boots? So I
can believe in Mr Ambler's fictional Colonel Haki and his
ambition to write a detective story, while I find it hard to
believe in the real Colonel Baden-Powell on a butterfly-
hunt in Dalmatia incorporating the plans of fortifications into
the pattern of his butterfly's wings. Bond's travelling equipment imagined by Mr Ian Fleming is certainly no more
fantastic than the furnishings of Herr Schellenberg's private
office. This is true, that is untrue, take your pick.

For the characters in one section, *A Gaggle of Suspects*, I
feel a personal sympathy, for there was an uncomfortable
month during the winter of 1951 in Indo-China when I too
found myself under suspicion. (Little did I realise that I was
in such distinguished company—Wordsworth and Lawrence,
Gauguin and Thomas Mann.) Some days passed before I
realised what lay behind the literary interests of a member of
the Sûreté stationed in Hanoi. Day by day he combed the
bookshops for copies of my novels, and in the evening he
would present himself with his little pile of books, seeking
dédicaces for himself, for his wife, for his friends. At last I
realised he was not the 'fan' I had been vain enough to believe:

he was trying inconspicuously to carry out the directions of the Commander-in-Chief, General de Lattre, who had on one embarrassing occasion and at his own dinner-table accused me of espionage. I was able after that to save M. 'Dupont' further trouble. We arranged to meet in the evenings for a drink and a game of *quatre-cent-vingt-et-un* at the Café de la Paix where I would tell him what I had been doing during the day. The courtesy of the Sûreté demanded that the guest —and suspect—should always win: the courtesy of the suspect demanded that the drinks should be equally divided. Unfortunately my police agent was unaccustomed to anything stronger than vermouth-cassis, and his wife refused to believe it was only duty which kept him up late and sent him home under so unaccustomed an influence. I still feel a sense of guilt towards my friendly watcher when I remember that sad tired bloodhound face, apparently sprung from some spiritual liaison between M. Fernandel and Mrs Browning, lifted from the glass he didn't want to drink, to listen to the story he didn't want to hear, apprehensive and reproachful. How merciless one can be when right is on one's side. He had a weak heart and there was an occasion when he passed completely out. Perhaps it was to quiet the memory of that kindly ineffective ghost that I have joined with my brother to compile *The Spy's Bedside Book* and to evoke figures far more absurd and improbable.

GRAHAM GREENE

1. A MISSION IS PROPOSED

I HAD just finished breakfast and was filling my pipe when I got Bullivant's telegram. It was at Furling, the big country house in Hampshire where I had come to convalesce after Loos, and Sandy, who was in the same case, was hunting for the marmalade. I flung him the flimsy with the blue strip pasted down on it, and he whistled.

"Hullo, Dick, you've got the battalion. Or maybe it's a staff billet. You'll be a blighted brass-hat, coming it heavy over the hard-working regimental officer. And to think of the language you've wasted on brass-hats in your time!"

I sat and thought for a bit, for that name "Bullivant" carried me back eighteen months to the hot summer before the war. I had not seen the man since, though I had read about him in the papers. For more than a year I had been a busy battalion officer, with no other thought than to hammer a lot of raw stuff into good soldiers. I had succeeded pretty well, and there was no prouder man on earth than Richard Hannay when he took his Lennox Highlanders over the parapets on that glorious and bloody 25th day of September. Loos was no picnic, and we had had some ugly bits of scrapping before that, but the worst bit of the campaign I had seen was a tea-party to the show I had been in with Bullivant before the war started.

The sight of his name on a telegram form seemed to change all my outlook on life. I had been hoping for the command of the battalion, and looking forward to being in at the finish with Brother Boche. But this message jerked my thoughts on to a new road. There might be other things in the war than straightforward fighting. Why on earth should the Foreign

Office want to see an obscure Major of the New Army and want to see him in double-quick time?

"I'm going up to town by the ten train," I announced; "I'll be back in time for dinner."

"Try my tailor," said Sandy. "He's got a very nice taste in red tabs. You can use my name."

An idea struck me. "You're pretty well all right now. If I wire for you, will you pack your own kit and mine and join me?"

"Right-o! I'll accept a job on your staff if they give you a corps. If so be as you come down tonight, be a good chap and bring a barrel of oysters from Sweeting's."

I travelled up to London in a regular November drizzle, which cleared up about Wimbledon to watery sunshine. I never could stand London during the war. It seemed to have lost its bearings and broken out into all manner of badges and uniforms which did not fit in with my notion of it. One felt the war more in its streets than in the field, or rather one felt the confusion of war without feeling the purpose. I dare say it was all right; but since August 1914 I never spent a day in town without coming home depressed to my boots.

I took a taxi and drove straight to the Foreign Office. Sir Walter did not keep me waiting long. But when his secretary took me to his room I would not have recognised the man I had known eighteen months before.

His big frame seemed to have dropped flesh and there was a stoop in the square shoulders. His face had lost its rosiness and was red in patches, like that of a man who gets too little fresh air. His hair was much greyer and very thin about the temples, and there were lines of overwork below the eyes. But the eyes were the same as before, keen and kindly and shrewd, and there was no change in the firm set of the jaw.

"We must on no account be disturbed for the next hour,"

he told his secretary. When the young man had gone he went across to both doors and turned the keys in them.

"Well, Major Hannay," he said, flinging himself into a chair beside the fire. "How do you like soldiering?"

"Right enough," I said, "though this isn't just the kind of war I would have picked myself. It's a comfortless, bloody business. But we've got the measure of the old Boche now, and it's dogged as does it. I count on getting back to the Front in a week or two."

"Will you get the battalion?" he asked. He seemed to have followed my doings pretty closely.

"I believe I've a good chance. I'm not in this show for honour and glory, though. I want to do the best I can, but I wish to Heaven it was over. All I think of is coming out of it with a whole skin."

He laughed. "You do yourself an injustice. What about the forward observation post at the Lone Tree? You forgot about the whole skin then."

I felt myself getting red. "That was all rot," I said, "and I can't think who told you about it. I hated the job, but I had to do it to prevent my subalterns going to glory. They were a lot of fire-eating young lunatics. If I had sent one of them he'd have gone on his knees to Providence and asked for trouble."

Sir Walter was still grinning.

"I'm not questioning your caution. You have the rudiments of it, or our friends of the Black Stone would have gathered you in at our last merry meeting. I would question it as little as your courage. What exercises my mind is whether it is best employed in the trenches."

"Is the War Office dissatisfied with me?" I asked sharply.

"They are profoundly satisfied. They propose to give you command of your battalion. Presently, if you escape a stray bullet, you will no doubt be a Brigadier. It is a wonderful war

for youth and brains. But . . . I take it you are in this business
to serve your country, Hannay?"

"I reckon I am," I said. "I am certainly not in it for my
health."

He looked at my leg, where the doctors had dug out the
shrapnel fragments, and smiled quizzically. "Pretty fit
again?" he asked.

"Tough as a sjambok. I thrive on the racket and eat and
sleep like a schoolboy."

He got up and stood with his back to the fire, his eyes
staring abstractedly out of the window at the wintry park.

"It is a great game, and you are the man for it, no doubt.
But there are others who can play it, for soldiering today asks
for the average rather than the exception in human nature. It
is like a big machine where the parts are standardised. You
are fighting, not because you are short of a job, but because
you want to help England. How if you could help her better
than by commanding a battalion—or a brigade—or, if it
comes to that, a division? How if there is a thing which you
alone can do? Not some *embusqué* business in an office, but a
thing compared to which your fight at Loos was a Sunday-
school picnic. You are not afraid of danger? Well, in this job
you would not be fighting with an army around you, but
alone. You are fond of tackling difficulties? Well, I can give
you a task which will try all your powers. Have you anything
to say?"

My heart was beginning to thump uncomfortably. Sir
Walter was not the man to pitch a case too high.

"I am a soldier," I said, "and under orders."

"True; but what I am about to propose does not come by
any conceivable stretch within the scope of a soldier's duties.
I shall perfectly understand if you decline. You will be acting
as I should act myself—as any sane man would. I would not
press you for worlds. If you wish it, I will not even make the

proposal, but let you go here and now, and wish you good luck with your battalion. I do not wish to perplex a good soldier with impossible decisions."

This piqued me and put me on my mettle.

"I am not going to run away before the guns fire. Let me hear what you propose."

Sir Walter crossed to a cabinet, unlocked it with a key from his chain, and took a piece of paper from a drawer. It looked like an ordinary half-sheet of notepaper.

"I take it," he said, "that your travels have not extended to the East."

"No," I said, "barring a shooting trip in East Africa."

"Have you by any chance been following the present campaign there?"

"I've read the newspapers pretty regularly since I went to hospital. I've got some pals in the Mesopotamia show, and of course I'm keen to know what is going to happen at Gallipoli and Salonika. I gather that Egypt is pretty safe."

"If you will give me your attention for ten minutes I will supplement your newspaper reading."

Sir Walter lay back in an armchair and spoke to the ceiling. It was the best story, the clearest and the fullest, I had ever got of any bit of the war. He told me just how and why and when Turkey had left the rails. I heard about her grievances over our seizure of her ironclads, of the mischief the coming of the *Goeben* had wrought, of Enver and his precious Committee and the way they had got a cinch on the old Turk. When he had spoken for a bit, he began to question me.

"You are an intelligent fellow, and you will ask how a Polish adventurer, meaning Enver, and a collection of Jews and gipsies should have got control of a proud race. The ordinary man will tell you that it was German organisation backed up with German money and German arms. You will inquire again how, since Turkey is primarily a religious

power, Islam has played so small a part in it all. The Sheikh-
ul-Islam is neglected, and though the Kaiser proclaims a Holy
War and calls himself Hadji Mohammed Guilliamo, and says
the Hohenzollerns are descended from the Prophet, that seems
to have fallen pretty flat. The ordinary man again will answer
that Islam in Turkey is becoming a back number, and that
Krupp guns are the new gods. Yet—I don't know. I do not
quite believe in Islam becoming a back number."

"Look at it another way," he went on. "If it were Enver
and Germany alone dragging Turkey into a European war for
purposes that no Turk cared a rush about, we might expect to
find the regular army obedient, and Constantinople. But in
the provinces, where Islam is strong, there would be trouble.
Many of us counted on that. But we have been disappointed.
The Syrian army is as fanatical as the hordes of the Mahdi.
The Senussi have taken a hand in the game. The Persian
Moslems are threatening trouble. There is a dry wind blowing through the East, and the parched grasses wait the spark.
And the wind is blowing towards the Indian border. Whence
comes that wind, think you?"

Sir Walter had lowered his voice and was speaking very
slow and distinct. I could hear the rain dripping from the
eaves of the window, and far off the hoot of taxis in Whitehall.

"Have you an explanation, Hannay?" he asked again.

"It looks as if Islam had a bigger hand in the thing than we
thought," I said. "I fancy religion is the only thing to knit
up such a scattered empire."

"You are right," he said. "You must be right. We have
laughed at the Holy War, the Jehad that old Von der Goltz
prophesied. But I believe that stupid old man with the big
spectacles was right. There is a Jehad preparing. The question is, how?"

"I'm hanged if I know," I said; "but I'll bet it won't be
done by a pack of stout German officers in *Pickelhaubes*. I

fancy you can't manufacture Holy Wars out of Krupp guns alone and a few staff officers and a battle-cruiser with her boilers burst."

"Agreed. They are not fools, however much we try to persuade ourselves of the contrary. But supposing they had got some tremendous sacred sanction—some holy thing, some book or gospel or some new prophet from the desert, something which would cast over the whole ugly mechanism of German war the glamour of the old torrential raids which crumpled the Byzantine Empire and shook the walls of Vienna? Islam is a fighting creed, and the mullah still stands in the pulpit with the Koran in one hand and a drawn sword in the other. Supposing there is some Ark of the Covenant which will madden the remotest Moslem peasant with dreams of Paradise? What then, my friend?"

"Then there will be hell let loose in those parts pretty soon."

"Hell which may spread. Beyond Persia, remember, lies India."

"You keep to suppositions. How much do you know?" I asked.

"Very little, except the fact. But the fact is beyond dispute. I have reports from agents everywhere—pedlars in South Russia, Afghan horse-dealers, Turcoman merchants, pilgrims on the road to Mecca, sheikhs in North Africa, sailors on the Black Sea coasters, sheep-skinned Mongols, Hindu fakirs, Greek traders in the Gulf, as well as respectable Consuls who use cyphers. They tell the same story. The East is waiting for a revelation. It has been promised one. Some star—man, prophecy, or trinket—is coming out of the West. The Germans know, and that is the card with which they are going to astonish the world."

"And the mission you spoke of for me is to go and find out?"

He nodded gravely. "That is the crazy and impossible mission."

"Tell me one thing, Sir Walter," I said. "I know it is the fashion in this country if a man has special knowledge to set him to some job exactly the opposite. I know all about Damaraland, but instead of being put on Botha's staff, as I applied to be, I was kept in Hampshire mud till the campaign in German South West Africa was over. I know a man who could pass as an Arab, but do you think they would send him to the East? They left him in my battalion—a lucky thing for me, for he saved my life at Loos. I know the fashion, but isn't this just carrying it a bit too far? There must be thousands of men who have spent years in the East and talk any language. They're the fellows for this job. I never saw a Turk in my life except a chap who did wrestling turns in a show at Kimberley. You've picked about the most useless man on earth."

"You've been a mining-engineer, Hannay," Sir Walter said. "If you wanted a man to prospect for gold in Barotse-land you would of course like to get one who knew the country and the people and the language. But the first thing you would require in him would be that he had a nose for finding gold and knew his business. That is the position now. I believe that you have a nose for finding out what our enemies try to hide. I know that you are brave and cool and resourceful. That is why I tell you the story. Besides . . ."

He unrolled a big map of Europe on the wall.

"I can't tell you where you'll get on the track of the secret, but I can put a limit to the quest. You won't find it east of the Bosphorus—not yet. It is still in Europe. It may be in Con-stantinople, or in Thrace. It may be farther west. But it is moving eastwards. If you are in time you may cut into its march to Constantinople. That much I can tell you. The secret is known in Germany, too, to those whom it concerns. It is in Europe that the seeker must search—at present."

"Tell me more," I said. "You can give me no details and no instructions. Obviously you can give me no help if I come to grief."

He nodded. "You would be beyond the pale."

"You give me a free hand?"

"Absolutely. You can have what money you like, and you can get what help you like. You can follow any plan you fancy, and go anywhere you think fruitful. We can give no directions."

"One last question. You say it is important. Tell me just how important."

"It is life and death," he said solemnly. "I can put it no higher and no lower. Once we know what is the menace we can meet it. As long as we are in the dark it works unchecked and we may be too late. The war must be won or lost in Europe. Yes; but if the East blazes up, our effort will be distracted from Europe and the great *coup* may fail. The stakes are no less than victory and defeat, Hannay."

I got out of my chair and walked to the window. It was a difficult moment in my life. I was happy in my soldiering; above all, happy in the company of my brother officers. I was asked to go off into the enemy's lands on a quest for which I believed I was manifestly unfitted—a business of lonely days and nights, of nerve-racking strain, of deadly peril shrouding me like a garment. Looking out on the bleak weather I shivered. It was too grim a business, too inhuman for flesh and blood. But Sir Walter had called it a matter of life and death, and I had told him that I was out to serve my country. He could not give me orders, but was I not under orders— higher orders than my Brigadier's? I thought myself incompetent, but cleverer men than me thought me competent, or at least competent enough for a sporting chance. I knew in my soul that if I declined I should never be quite at peace in the world again. And yet Sir Walter had called the scheme madness, and said that he himself would never have accepted.

How does one make a great decision? I swear that when I turned round to speak I meant to refuse. But my answer was Yes, and I had crossed the Rubicon. My voice sounded cracked and far away.

Sir Walter shook hands with me and his eyes blinked a little.

"I may be sending you to your death, Hannay—Good God, what a damned task-mistress duty is!—If so, I shall be haunted with regrets, but *you* will never repent. Have no fear of that. You have chosen the roughest road, but it goes straight to the hill-tops."

He handed me the half-sheet of notepaper. On it were written three words—"*Kasredin*", "*cancer*" and "*v.I.*"

"That is the only clue we possess," he said. "I cannot construe it, but I can tell you the story. We have had our agents working in Persia and Mesopotamia for years—mostly young officers of the Indian Army. They carry their lives in their hands, and now and then one disappears, and the sewers of Bagdad might tell a tale. But they find out many things, and they count the game worth the candle. They have told us of the star rising in the West, but they could give us no details. All but one—the best of them. He had been working between Mosul and the Persian frontier as a muleteer, and had been south, into the Bakhtiari hills. He found out something, but his enemies knew that he knew and he was pursued. Three months ago, just before Kut, he staggered into Delamain's camp with ten bullet-holes in him and a knife slash on his forehead. He mumbled his name, but beyond that and the fact that there was a Something coming from the West he told them nothing. He died in ten minutes. They found this paper on him, and since he cried out the word "Kasredin" in his last moments, it must have had something to do with his quest. It is for you to find out if it has any meaning."

I folded it up and placed it in my pocket-book.

"What a great fellow! What was his name?" I asked.

Sir Walter did not answer at once. He was looking out of the window. "His name," he said at last, "was Harry Bullivant. He was my son. God rest his brave soul!"

JOHN BUCHAN

2. DIRECTIVE TO COLONEL ZABOTIN

[Grant was the cover-name for Colonel Zabotin, Soviet Military Attaché in Ottawa. Alek was the cover-name for Dr Allan Nunn May. Director was the Director of Military Intelligence in Moscow.]

To Grant

THE arrangements worked out for the meeting are not satisfactory. I am informing you of new ones.

1. *Place*: In front of the British Museum in London, on Great Russell Street, at the opposite side of the street, about Museum Street, from the side of Tottenham Court Road repeat Tottenham Court Road, Alek walks from Tottenham Court Road, the contact man from the opposite side—Southampton Row.

2. *Time*: As indicated by you, however, it would be more expedient to carry out the meeting at 20 o'clock, if it should be convenient to Alek, as at 23 o'clock it is too dark. As for the time, agree about it with Alek and communicate the decision to me. In case the meeting should not take place in October, the time and day will be repeated in the following months.

3. *Identification signs*: Alek will have under his left arm the newspaper *Times*, the contact man will have in his left hand the magazine *Picture Post*.

4. *The Password*: The contact man: "What is the shortest way to the Strand?"

Alek: "Well, come along. I am going that way."

In the beginning of the business conversation Alek says: "Best regards from Mikel."

Report on transmitting the conditions to Alek.

DIRECTOR

3. A DAMNED GOOD STORY

THE Colonel, who was known in the Intelligence Department, as Ashenden later discovered, by the letter R., rose when he came in and shook hands with him. He was a man somewhat above the middle height, lean, with a yellow, deeply-lined face, thin grey hair and a toothbrush moustache. The thing immediately noticeable about him was the closeness with which his blue eyes were set. He only just escaped a squint. They were hard and cruel eyes, and very wary; and they gave him a cunning, shifty look. Here was a man that you could neither like nor trust at first sight. His manner was pleasant and cordial.

He asked Ashenden a good many questions and then, without further to-do, suggested that he had particular qualifications for the secret service. Ashenden was acquainted with several European languages and his profession was excellent cover; on the pretext that he was writing a book he could without attracting attention visit any neutral country. It was while they were discussing this point that R. said:

"You know you ought to get material that would be very useful to you in your work."

"I shouldn't mind that," said Ashenden.

"I'll tell you an incident that occurred only the other day

and I can vouch for its truth. I thought at the time it would make a damned good story. One of the French ministers went down to Nice to recover from a cold and he had some very important documents with him that he kept in a dispatch-case. They were very important indeed. Well, a day or two after he arrived he picked up a yellow-haired lady at some restaurant or other where there was dancing, and he got very friendly with her. To cut a long story short, he took her back to his hotel—of course it was a very imprudent thing to do—and when he came to himself in the morning the lady and the dispatch-case had disappeared. They had one or two drinks up in his room, and his theory is that when his back was turned the woman slipped a drug into his glass."

R. finished and looked at Ashenden with a gleam in his close-set eyes.

"Dramatic, isn't it?" he asked.

"Do you mean to say that happened the other day?"

"The week before last."

"Impossible," cried Ashenden. "Why, we've been putting that incident on the stage for sixty years, we've written it in a thousand novels. Do you mean to say that life has only just caught up with us?"

R. was a trifle disconcerted.

"Well, if necessary, I could give you names and dates, and believe me, the Allies have been put to no end of trouble by the loss of the documents that the dispatch-case contained."

"Well, sir, if you can't do better than that in the secret service," sighed Ashenden, "I'm afraid that as a source of inspiration to the writer of fiction it's a washout. We really *can't* write that story much longer."

W. SOMERSET MAUGHAM

4. A LATE CALL AT THE GERMAN EMBASSY

In a deep armchair next to one of the table lamps a man was seated, in such a way that his face was in shadow. He sat so still that he might have been sleeping. . . .

I guessed that he was in his early fifties. He had thick black hair, brushed straight back from his forehead, which was fairly high. His dark eyes kept darting nervously from me to the door and back again. His chin was firm, his nose small and shapeless. Not an attractive face on the whole. Later, after I'd seen a great deal of him, it occurred to me to compare his face to that of a clown without his make-up on—the face of a man accustomed to disguising his true feelings.

There was a moment's silence, probably not so long as it seemed to me, while we eyed one another.

"Who on earth can he be?" I thought. "He's certainly not a member of the Diplomatic Corps."

I sat down and motioned him to do the same. Instead he tiptoed to the door, jerked it open, shut it silently again, and came back to resume his seat in the armchair with evident relief. At that moment he really did seem a strange sort of character.

Then, haltingly at first, and in his poor French, he began to speak:

"I have an offer to make you, a proposition or whatever you call it, a proposition for the Germans. But before I tell you what it is I ask your word that whether you accept it or not you won't ever mention it to anyone except your chief. Any indiscretion on your part would make your life as worthless as mine. I'd see to that if it was the last thing I did."

As he said this he made an unpleasant but unmistakable gesture, passing his hand across his throat.

"Do you give me your word?"

"Of course I do. If I didn't know how to keep a secret I wouldn't be here now. Please be so good as to tell me what it is you want."

I made a show of looking at my wrist watch with some ostentation. He reacted at once.

"You'll have plenty of time for me once you know why I'm here. My proposition is of the utmost importance to your Government. I am . . ." He hesitated, and I wondered if it was due to his difficulty in expressing himself in French or whether he wished to test my reaction. ". . . I can give you extremely secret papers, the most secret that exist."

He paused again for a moment, and then added:

"They come straight from the British Embassy. Well? That would interest you, wouldn't it?"

I did my best to keep a poker face. My first thought was that he was a petty crook out for some easy money. I would have to be careful. He seemed to have guessed what I was thinking, for he said:

"But I'll want money for them, a lot of money. My work, you know, is dangerous, and if I were caught . . ."

He repeated the unpleasant gesture with his hand across his throat, though this time, at any rate, it was not meant for me.

"You've got funds for that sort of thing, haven't you? Or your Ambassador has? Your Government would provide it. I want twenty thousand pounds, English pounds sterling."

I offered him a cigarette which he accepted gratefully, taking a few deep pulls and then stubbing it out. He rose and went to the door once more to make sure that there was no one listening. Then he turned back and planted himself squarely in front of me. I got up too.

"You'd like to know who I am, wouldn't you? My name is quite unimportant and has no bearing. Perhaps I'll tell you what I do, but first listen to me. I'll give you three days to consider my proposition. You'll have to see your chief, and he'll probably have to get in touch with Berlin. On the 30th of October, at three in the afternoon, I'll telephone you at your office and ask you if you've received a letter for me. I'll call myself Pierre. If you say no, you'll never see me again. If you say yes, it'll mean that you've accepted my offer. In that case I'll come to see you again at ten o'clock on the evening of the same day. Not here though. We'll have to arrange some other meeting place. You'll then receive from me two rolls of film, containing photographs of British secret documents. I'll receive from you the sum of twenty thousand pounds in bank-notes. You'll be risking twenty thousand pounds, but I'll have risked my life. Should you approve of my first delivery you can have more. For each subsequent roll of film I'll want fifteen thousand pounds. Well?"

I was inclined to think that the offer might be genuine, but I was convinced that, in view of the exorbitant price he was asking, nothing could come of it, particularly since he seemed to expect us to buy the papers sight unseen. I made a mental note to stress the inordinate risk in the memo that I would have to write about all this. I was certain the offer would be turned down.

Nevertheless we agreed that he should telephone me at my office on the 30th day of October at three o'clock. We also agreed that in the event of his offer being accepted we would meet near the toolshed at the end of the Embassy garden.

After these details had been arranged he asked me to switch out all the lights in the hall and on the stairs. He wished to leave the house under cover of complete darkness.

I complied with his request. When I came back to the drawing-room he had put on his overcoat and his hat, which was pulled down low over his eyes. It was past midnight by now.

I stood at the door to let him pass. He suddenly gripped my arm, and hissed in my ear:

"You'd like to know who I am? I'm the British Ambassador's valet."

Without awaiting my reaction to this he stepped out into the darkness.

Thus ended my first meeting with the man who, a few days later, was given the code name of Cicero.

L. C. MOYZISCH

5. THE VALUE OF HIDE-AND-SEEK

THE game of hide-and-seek is really one of the best games for a boy, and can be elaborated until it becomes scouting in the field. It teaches you a lot.

I was strongly addicted to it as a child, and the craft learned in that innocent field of sport has stood me in good stead in many a critical time since. To lie flat in a furrow among the currant bushes when I had not time to reach the neighbouring box bushes before the pursuer came in sight taught me the value of not using the most obvious cover, since it would at once be searched. The hunters went at once to the box bushes as the likely spot, while I could watch their doings from among the stems of the currant bushes.

Often I have seen hostile scouts searching the obvious bits of cover, but they did not find *me* there; and, like the elephant hunter among the fern trees, or a boar in a cotton crop, so a boy in the currant bushes is invisible to the enemy, while he can watch every move of the enemy's legs.

This I found of value when I came to be pursued by mounted military police, who suspected me of being a spy at some manœuvres abroad.

SIR ROBERT BADEN-POWELL

6. TAKE A HARD-BOILED EGG

TAKE a spot of lemon juice. Use a perfectly clean nib. Dip it into the lemon and write the message on a piece of paper. Allow the juice to dry and there will be nothing to be seen. Run a hot iron over the paper and the writing will return—faint and light brown in shade.

*

Take a clean nib and dip it in water—or merely write with the dry nib on the paper. The nib will make minute scratches on the paper—invisible to the naked eye, but easily seen under the microscope. An iodine vapour bath can also be used. This is a simple apparatus—a tin oven in which iodine is maintained at the lowest temperature at which it will remain vapourised. The letter is introduced into the bath, and when it is withdrawn after a few minutes crystals of iodine will have settled along the tiny rough edges formed by the scratch of the nib.

*

Naphthol, collodion and acetone in the proportions of one, twenty, sixty. For the reagent, five grains of sulphuric acid are mixed with fifty cubic centimetres of nitric acid in a litre of water and added cold to one gramme of sodium nitrate. Fifty grammes of sodium acetate are then dissolved in two hundred cubic centimetres of water. The paper is dipped in a mixture of a hundred cubic centimetres of the first solution and twenty cubic centimetres of the second solution.

*

A mixture of brandy and milk.

*

Take a hard-boiled egg. Mix alum and vinegar together to the consistency of ink and write the message on the shell. As the ink dries there is nothing to be seen but a few hours later the message (which must be written in large letters) will appear on the white of the egg.   BERNARD NEWMAN

EXAMPLE OF INVISIBLE WRITING[1]

[1] By those under the age of eighteen this page should not be submitted to any alcoholic test.

Hazards of the Profession

They speak of murder . . . I can't trust anyone any more . . . assassination awaits me on the least suspicion. . . .

> FELIX STIDGER, Union counter-spy among the Copperheads in the American Civil War, in a scribbled report to his chief, Colonel Henry B. Carrington

7. TRICKED

BEFORE I could utter aught save a muffled curse, I was flung head first into an empty piano case, the heavy lid of which was instantly closed on me. . . . I had been tricked!

WILLIAM LE QUEUX

8. A WHIP OF THE CIRCASSIAN SORT

THEY kicked me to the head of the stairs, and stretched me over a guard-bench, pommelling me. Two knelt on my ankles, bearing down on the backs of my knees, while two more twisted my wrists till they cracked, and then crushed them and my neck against the wood. The corporal had run downstairs; and now came back with a whip of the Circassian sort, a thong of supple black hide, rounded, and tapering from the thickness of a thumb at the grip (which was wrapped in silver) down to a hard point finer than a pencil.

He saw me shivering, partly I think, with cold, and made it whistle over my ear, taunting me that before his tenth cut I would howl for mercy; and then he began to lash me madly across and across with all his might, while I locked my teeth to endure this thing which lapped itself like flaming wire about my body.

To keep my mind in control I numbered the blows, but after twenty lost count, and could feel only the shapeless weight of pain, not tearing claws, for which I had prepared, but a gradual cracking apart of my whole being by some too-great force whose waves rolled up my spine till they were pent within my brain, to clash terribly together. Somewhere in the place a cheap clock ticked loudly, and it distressed me that their beating was not in its time. I writhed and twisted, but was held so tightly that my struggles were useless. After the corporal ceased, the men took it up, very deliberately, giving me so many, and then an interval during which they would squabble for the next turn. This was repeated often, for what may have been no more than ten minutes. Always for the first of every new series, my head would be pulled round, to see how a hard white ridge, like a railway, darkening slowly into crimson, leaped over my skin at the instant of each stroke, with a bead of blood where two ridges crossed. As the punishment proceeded the whip fell more and more upon existing weals, biting blacker or more wet, till my flesh quivered with accumulated pain, and with terror of the next blow coming. They soon conquered my determination not to cry, but while my will ruled my lips I used only Arabic, and before the end a merciful sickness choked my utterance.

T. E. LAWRENCE

9. A NASTY SCRATCH

On the fourth night of our arrival in the French capital I returned to the hotel about midnight, having dined at the Café Américain with Greville, the naval attaché at the Embassy. In washing my hands prior to turning in, I received a nasty scratch on my left wrist from a pin which a careless laundress had left in the towel. There was a little blood, but I tied my handkerchief around it, and, tired out, lay down and was soon asleep.

Half an hour afterwards, however, I was aroused by an

excruciating pain over my whole left side, a strange twitching of the muscles of my face and hands, and a contraction of the throat which prevented me from breathing or crying out.

I tried to rise and press the electric bell for assistance, but could not. My whole body seemed entirely paralysed. Then the ghastly truth flashed upon me, causing me to break out into a cold sweat.

That pin had been placed there purposely. I had been poisoned.

WILLIAM LE QUEUX

10. A SPY ADVERTISES

To anyone whom it may concern: I think it advisable to state that I have no documents of any importance in my own possession in connection with any other country or work I have undertaken. I am making this statement as, on January 4th, 1938, a friend and I left a certain Embassy in London. We were followed to Victoria Station, where I caught the 5.35 train. From then on, my memory is a blank until I found myself in hospital the following morning. Some papers of mine were missing. I will let the *Mid-Sussex Times* complete the story:

ACCIDENT IN MID-SUSSEX
Mr W. H. Greene, of Oak Cottage, Plumpton, is in the Haywards Heath Hospital suffering from head injuries sustained in a motor accident at Plumpton last week. He was found lying unconscious near his damaged car.

HERBERT GREENE

11. A BATHROOM AT THE PARIS RITZ

HE seized me by the collar and dragged me across the floor to my bathroom. I didn't even struggle because I thought he was only going to lock me in, but not a bit of it—he took the cord off my dressing-gown and started to make a noose.

Can you imagine what I felt like then? I realised with a horrible suddenness that he really meant to do me in. I sat on the floor there thinking desperately—racking my brains for some idea that would literally save my neck. I began to talk again—quickly, feverishly, of the first thing that came into my head, anything to gain time.

His only reply was to stoop down and seize me by the nose—then with his free hand he thrust a sponge into my mouth. That ended the conversation, of course, and I could only flap helplessly about on the floor like a fresh-caught salmon on the bank.

He slid the cord over the hook on the door—fixed the noose round my neck, tested the knot—and then began to hoist!

God! it was a horrible business. I dug my chin down into my chest as hard as I could, but I felt myself being drawn up in steady jerks.

Suddenly I left the ground and the cord tightened round my neck—the hook hit me on the back of the head as he gave a last heave on the cord—and there I was, dangling in the air while he lashed the end of it to the door-knob.

He supported my weight for a moment while he undid the cord that bound my hands to my sides and the curtain sash that tied my feet—then he let me drop.

The second my hands were free I was clawing at my neck, but the noose was tight about it and I couldn't get my fingers in. I couldn't shout because the sponge was in my mouth, and even when I wrenched it out I could only gurgle horribly.

Through a haze of pain and dizziness I could see Essenbach as he stood there studying me with cold deliberation. Then he tipped the bathroom chair over just out of my reach and I heard him say:

"Suicide—suicide of Colonel Thornton." After that he left me.

DENNIS WHEATLEY

12. A TRUSSED FOWL

SCARCE had I touched the seat when, of its own accord, it tipped backwards and my legs went high into the air. It seemed set upon a pivot, so that anyone, seating themselves in it, would be thrown entirely off their balance.

I grasped the air in wild indignity, but ere I could realise what had happened the two ruffians, who had sprung forward, had slipped cords upon my wrists and ankles, and next second I found myself bound to the seat hand and foot.

'What do you mean by this, you scoundrels!" I shouted in anger.

But the pair only laughed aloud at my helplessness.

"What have I done that you should hold me thus?" I demanded, in an instant realising that I had fallen into a trap.

"Look sharp!" cried the man who had admitted me. "See that he is secure. We must fly while there is yet time!"

"Time for what?" I asked.

"Time for us to escape," replied the man with the beetling brows. Then he added quickly, with a sinister laugh, "See that lamp upon the table? Well, within is a powerful explosive. Three minutes from now the oil will be exhausted and then it will explode, and you, together with this house, will be blown to atoms!"

"You fiends!" I shrieked, glancing at the innocent-looking table-lamp, "then you intend that I shall die! This is a dastardly plot." I struggled frantically to free myself. The chair had not, however, recovered its proper position, and my legs, being up in the air, rendered me entirely helpless.

I lay like a trussed fowl while the two hired assassins laughed in my face.

"Quick!" cried the beetle-browed man to his companion, "let us get out of it!" And they both hurriedly left, locking the door behind them—left me there to my terrible fate!

I was horrified. I shouted for help, but to my appeal came no response. My eyes were fixed upon that fatal lamp. It seemed to possess a weird fascination for me. Only a few moments remained, and I should be hurled into eternity.

WILLIAM LE QUEUX

13. IN THE BACK OF THE HEAD

IT was on the very eve of our departure that I received a signal from Moscow marked "Top Secret and Priority". I decoded it personally and took it at once to the Chief of Staff, Voitenkov. The C.O., General Kraft, had left for the Soviet Union that afternoon. Voitenkov spread it out on his desk and his eyebrows twitched a little. He nodded, but said nothing.

The signal read: "Render harmless Agent 063, found to be a British spy."

Now Agent 063 was no ordinary agent. Before I left Moscow I had decoded many reports supplied by him which were of the highest value to the Soviet Union. Agent 063, I discovered when I arrived in Sinkiang, was actually the Chinese Governor of Yarkand, a huge man who could hardly squeeze his fat legs into an ordinary chair. He was a well-known figure to most of us, and came frequently to our headquarters with his adjutant to visit General Kraft. On these occasions he wore Chinese-style trousers, top-boots which had to be specially made for him, and a light leather civilian top-coat. Owing to his eminence, he met all important visitors to the district, and was able to supply us with a mass of inside information about missionaries, traders and others who were said to be carrying on pro-British propaganda. There is no doubt that Agent 063 had given immense help to the Soviet expedition. It is also certain that he had acquired an intimate and accurate knowledge of our activities.

As for the rest of the signal, "render harmless" is a recognised formula used in secret communications with places outside the Soviet Union; it simply means "execute".

Voitenkov quickly drew up a plan to implement Moscow's instructions. A Chinese interpreter whom we knew as "Peter" and who was on good terms with the Governor, was at once sent to invite him to visit our headquarters that evening, as General Kraft wished to say good-bye before his return to the Soviet Union. It was not likely that the Governor would refuse such an invitation from the Soviet Commander, and he duly appeared.

As soon as he entered he was seized and bound, and was taken to the interrogator's room. The interrogation lasted about fifteen minutes. Though I was not present I later saw the brief interrogation report, which indicated that Agent 063 had been accused of being a British spy but had denied it. Apparently he had been completely dumbfounded by the charge and by the speed of events.

Meanwhile three of my wireless operators had been given the task of digging a large grave in the earth floor of the corridor outside our office.

Agent 063 was carried out, his mouth gagged and his hands

bound behind his back and was laid face downwards in the corridor alongside the grave. While the engine of a motor-truck in the nearby courtyard was accelerated with tremendous din, one of the interrogator's assistants fired three revolver shots into the back of his head. Above the noise of the truck engine I heard the sound that came from him as the bullets were fired into him. It was something between a long gasp and groan; I will not easily forget the sound. His great bulk was then rolled into the grave and petrol was poured over him and set alight to make his body unrecognizable. Then the earth was filled in and stamped down again, and the bamboo mats were replaced in the corridors.

It was my concluding task to report to Moscow that their instructions concerning Agent 063 had been carried out to the letter.

> VLADIMIR PETROV, describing his experiences
> with the O.G.P.U. in the Chinese province
> of Sinkiang in 1937

14. A LITTLE BLACK BERET

DR HERMAN GOERTZ, a lieutenant on the reserve of the Luftwaffe, was dropped by parachute in County Meath on the night of 5/6 May 1940. He was fifty years old and in 1936 had been sentenced to four years' imprisonment for spying, conscientiously but not very usefully, on RAF airfields. In Maidstone gaol, where he served his sentence, he met several members of the Irish Republican Army. His mission in 1940, which seems to have been loosely if at all defined, had some connection with an unpractical plan, code-named *Kathleen*, for a German invasion of Ireland; this had been submitted to the *Abwehr* in Hamburg by an emissary of the IRA.

Goertz was dropped—in the wrong place—wearing German uniform and carrying military identity papers made out in a false name. He failed to recover the parachute and container with his wireless set and other equipment in it, and set off to walk to a rendezvous in County Wicklow, seventy miles away. He swam the River Boyne "with", as he afterwards wrote, "great difficulty since the weight of my fur combination exhausted me. This swim also cost me the loss of my invisible ink." Soon, exhausted by hunger and strain, he was in worse case, and discarded his uniform; "I was now in high boots, breeches and jumper, with a little black beret on my head. . . . I kept my military cap as a vessel for drinks and my war medals for sentimental reasons. . . . I had no Irish money and did not realise that I could use English money quite freely."

Although with Irish help he established wireless contact with Germany and was not arrested by the Irish police until November 1941, Goertz—out of depth in the intricate crosscurrents of IRA politics—achieved nothing. In 1947, when told that he was to be repatriated to Germany, he took poison; the reasons for his suicide are not known. . . . The lonely, brave, baffled figure trudging across the empty Irish landscape in jackboots, with a little black beret on his head and a pocket full of 1914–18 medals, is a reminder of how far the German intelligence effort fell short of those standards of subtlety and dissimulation which were expected of it. . . .

PETER FLEMING

15. AT THE SOCIAL CLUB

To the casual glance of the passer-by, there was nothing to differentiate him from any other young fellow of his apparent age and station; and, therefore, it was quite out of the question that the policeman who was beginning his night's work by flashing his bull's-eye into the doorways, and trying door handles and shop shutters, should bestow more than a passing glance, quite devoid of interest, upon him as he strode by. He was sober and respectable, and seemingly making his way quietly home after a decently spent Saturday evening.

There was nothing to tell the guardian of the peace that the most dangerous man in Europe was passing within a few feet of him, or that if only he could have arrested him on some valid pretext that would have enabled him to lock him up for the rest of the night, and then handed him over to the Criminal Investigation Department at New Scotland Yard—the officers of which had been hunting for just such a man as he for the last twelve months—he would have prevented the commission of a crime which, within twenty-four hours, was to plunge a whole nation into panic and mourning, and send a thrill of horror through Europe. . . .

In St Petersburg, or even in Paris, such a man would have been shadowed, his every movement would have been watched, all his comings and goings noticed, and at any moment—such a one as this, for instance—he might have been pounced upon and searched as a suspicious person; and assuredly, if he had been, the toils of the law would have closed about him in such fashion that little but a miracle could have set him free again.

But here in London, the asylum of anarchy, and the focus of the most dangerous forces in the world, he went on his way unquestioned and unsuspected, for, although the police were morally certain that such a man existed, they had no idea as to his personality, no notion that this smart, good-looking young fellow, whose name had never been heard in connection even with such anarchist clubs as were known to have their quarters in London, and much less, therefore, with any of the crimes that had been laid to the charge of anarchy, was in reality even a greater criminal than Vaillant or Henry, or even the infamous Ravachol himself.

These were only the blind if willing tools, the instruments of political murder, the visible hands that obeyed the unseen brain, those who did the work and paid the penalty. But Max Renault was the brain itself, the intellect which conceived the plans for the execution of which the meaner and cheaper disciples of the sanguinary brotherhood of the knife and the bomb died on the scaffold, or wore out their lives in penal prisons or the mines of Siberia.

In a word, he was the moving spirit and directing intellect of what was soon to become the most dreaded body of men and women in the world, but which was now only known to the initiated as "Autonomie Group Number 7" . . .

A few hundred yards past the top of the hill, Max turned sharply to the left, walked along a side street, turned to the right at the end of this, and went into another. Three minutes' quick walking brought him to the side door of a house which had a small timber yard on one side of it, and on the other a deserted beer-house, which had lost its licence, and remained unoccupied because the premises were fit for no other kind of business.

The house itself had a low shop front, with the lower half of its windows painted a dull green, and on the upper part was an arc of white letters making the legend "Social Club and Eclectic Institute". A lamp over the shop door bore the same inscription in white letters on blue glass, but the lamp was out now, for it was one of the rules of the club that all members should leave the premises not later than twelve o'clock at night on week-days and half-past eleven on Sundays.

This rule, however, seemed only to apply to a certain section of the members. After Max had opened the side door with his latch-key, and ascended the stairs at the end of the passage, with a familiarity that enabled him to dispense with a light in the absolute darkness, he knocked at the door of an upstairs room which he found without the slightest hesitation. It was opened, and he found himself in the presence of four men and three women sitting round a table on which were the remains of what had evidently been a substantial and even luxurious supper.

Renault's action on entering the room was one which more than bore out what has been said of his character and the desperate work that he was engaged in. He acknowledged with a brief, curt nod the salutations of the company, and then, putting his back against the door, he pulled his right hand out of his trousers pocket, and said, in a quiet, almost well-bred voice, which had just the faintest trace of a foreign accent:

"Victor Berthauld, sit still!"

There was a small, slender-barrelled, six-chambered Colt in his hand, and the muzzle was pointed at a little lean, wiry, black-muzzled, close-cropped Frenchman, who had begun to wriggle uneasily in his seat the moment Max had made his appearance. His black eyes rolling in their deep sockets took one frightened glance from face to face, and then he said, in a voice to which he in vain tried to impart a tone of bravado:

"Well, Comrade Renault, what do you want with me, and what is that revolver drawn for?"

"Don't 'comrade' me, you little rat," said Max, with a short, savage laugh. "Tell me who tried to warn the Paris police that Carnot's life was in danger. Tell me who would have had Santo arrested at Marseilles if his telegram had only got into the hands it was intended for.

"Tell me who means to repeat the message tomorrow morning to Paris and Lyons, and who means to have this place raided by the English police at an inconvenient hour within the next week, on the ground of unlawful gambling being permitted here. Tell me that, you dirty hound, and then I'll tell you, if you don't know, what we usually do with traitors."

Berthauld sat for a moment speechless with fear. Then, with an imprecation on his lips, he leapt to his feet. Not a hand was moved to restrain him, but as he rose to his full height, Renault's arm straightened out, there was a crack and a flash, and a little puff of plaster reduced to dust leapt out of the angle of the wall behind him; but before the bullet struck the wall, it had passed through his forehead and out at the back of his head, his body shrank together and collapsed in a huddled heap in his chair, and Max, putting his pistol back into his pocket, said, just as quietly as before:

"It's a curious thing that even among eight of us we must have a traitor. I hope there aren't any more about. Take that thing down to the cellar, and then let us get to business; I've something important to tell you."

So saying, he walked round the table to a vacant armchair that stood at the end opposite the door, threw himself back in it, took out a cigar and lit it, and, with the same unshaken hand that a moment before had taken a fellow-creature's life, poured out a tumblerful of champagne from a bottle that stood half-empty beside him. . . .

"I hope I haven't shocked you by such a rough-and-ready administration of justice," said Max, half-turning in his chair and addressing a girl who sat next to him on his right hand.

"No," said the girl. "It was obviously necessary. If half you charged him with is true, he ought to have been crucified, let alone shot. I can't think what such vermin are made for."

And as she spoke, she flicked the ash off a cigarette that she held between her fingers, put it between as dainty a pair of lips as ever were made for kissing, and sent a delicate little blue wreathing cloud up to mingle with the haze that filled the upper part of the room. GEORGE GRIFFITH

16. "THAT INDEED IS TO DIE"

"Humph!" ejaculated the pedlar; "there is something particular indeed to be seen behind the thicket on our left—turn your head a little, and you may see and profit by it too."

Henry eagerly seized this permission to look aside, and the blood curdled to his heart as he observed that they were passing a gallows, that unquestionably had been erected for his own execution—he turned his face from the sight in undisguised horror.

"There is a warning to be prudent in that bit of wood," said the pedlar, in the sententious manner that he often adopted.

"It is a terrific sight, indeed!" cried Henry, for a moment veiling his eyes with his hand, as if to drive a vision from before him.

The pedlar moved his body partly around, and spoke with energetic but gloomy bitterness—"and yet, Captain Wharton, you see it where the setting sun shines full upon you; the air you breathe is clear and fresh from the hills before you. Every step that you take leaves that hated gallows behind, and every dark hollow, and every shapeless rock in the mountains, offers you a hiding place from the vengeance of your enemies. But I have seen the gibbet raised, when no place of refuge offered. Twice have I been buried in dungeons where, fettered and in chains, I have passed nights in torture, looking forward to the morning's dawn that was to light me to a death of infamy. The sweat has started from limbs that seemed already drained of their moisture, and if I ventured to the hole that admitted air through grates of iron, to look out upon the smiles of nature, which God has bestowed for the meanest of his creatures, the gibbet has glared before my eyes, like an evil conscience harrowing the soul of a dying man. Four times have I been in their power, besides this last; but twice—twice—did I think that my hour had come. It is hard to die at the best, Captain Wharton; but to spend your last moments alone and unpitied, to know that none near you so much as think of the fate that is to you the closing of all that is earthly; to think, that in a few hours, you are to be led from the gloom, which as you dwell on what follows becomes dear to you, to the face of day, and there to meet all eyes upon you, as if you were a wild beast; and to lose sight of everything amidst the jeers and scoffs of your fellow-creatures. That, Captain Wharton, that indeed is to die!"

FENIMORE COOPER

17. SEDUCED WITH THE OLD TRICKS

CONTROL of the passes was, he saw, the key
To this new district, but who would get it?
He, the trained spy, had walked into the trap
For a bogus guide, seduced with the old tricks.

At Greenhearth was a fine site for a dam
And easy power, had they pushed the rail
Some stations nearer. They ignored his wires.
The bridges were unbuilt and trouble coming.

The street music seemed gracious now to one
For weeks up in the desert. Woken by water
Running away in the dark, he often had
Reproached the night for a companion
Dreamed of already. They would shoot, of course,
Parting easily who were never joined.

W. H. AUDEN

18. AN EXCELLENT BABADAGLY

FROM Rome to Petersburg is a far cry, especially in winter. You probably know Cubat's, that big, glaring restaurant in the Morskaya.

Everyone who has been in the Russian capital knows it, and many have, no doubt, regaled themselves with a dish of exquisite sterlet direct from the Volga, for there are only two places in the world where that delicacy can be obtained in perfection, at the Ermitage at Moscow and at Cubat's.

On the night of the 5th of March I was seated alone at one of the many small tables of the restaurant, and having dined well was sipping my kümmel, smoking an excellent Babadagly—that brand of cigarette that one cannot obtain outside the Russian Empire—and pretending to be interested in the "latest informations" in the *Novoe Vremya*. I say pretending, for all my attention was really concentrated upon the movements of two persons, an elderly grey-bearded man and a young and rather pretty woman who, seated opposite me, were also dining. The place was crowded, but the pair, entering after me, managed to find a seat almost opposite. Both were well dressed, the woman wearing rich heavy furs of Zinovieff's cut, which became her well, and when on seating herself she allowed them to slip off she displayed a neat figure and a smart evening gown of some soft turquoise stuff cut slightly low, while about the throat was a thin gold chain to which, uncut and set as a pendant, was attached one of those dark green Siberian stones that are so often worn by Russian women.

She was decidedly pretty, with dark hair, regular features, well-defined brows, and a pair of sparkling eyes that danced mischievously whenever they glanced at me. Her companion, however, was a rather evil-looking, square-jawed fellow who apparently treated her without consideration, for he ordered from the menu without consulting her.

They had been sitting there for nearly three-quarters of an hour, and I had become quite fascinated by the pale, wistful face of the pretty woman before me, when a newspaper hawker, well muffled up in his ragged *shuba*, entered from the street, and passing from one table to another came at last to mine.

"This is for you," he said quickly in Russian. "Give me five copeks and attract no attention. Look in the margin." And taking a paper from his bundle he laid it upon the table.

In surprise I flung the coin upon the table, and taking up the newspaper saw some faint writing in pencil on the margin close to the heavily-printed heading. The words were in French, and written in a strange hand, evidently that of a Russian. They read:

"Beware of Nicholas Levitski and Pauline Ozeroff who are sitting opposite you. They are agents of Secret Police."

WILLIAM LE QUEUX

19. I SPY

CHARLIE STOWE waited until he heard his mother snore before he got out of bed. Even then he moved with caution and tip-toed to the window. The front of the house was irregular, so that it was possible to see a light burning in his mother's room. But now all the windows were dark. A searchlight passed across the sky, lighting the banks of cloud and probing the dark deep spaces between, seeking enemy airships. The wind blew from the sea, and Charlie Stowe could hear behind his mother's snores the beating of the waves. A draught through the cracks in the window-frame stirred his nightshirt. Charlie Stowe was frightened.

But the thought of the tobacconist's shop which his father kept down a dozen wooden stairs drew him on. He was twelve years old, and already boys at the County School mocked him because he had never smoked a cigarette. The packets were piled twelve deep below, Gold Flake and Players, De Reszke, Abdulla, Woodbines, and the little shop lay under a thin haze of stale smoke which would completely disguise his crime. That it was a crime to steal some of his father's stock Charlie Stowe had no doubt, but he did not love his father; his father was unreal to him, a wraith, pale, thin, indefinite, who noticed him only spasmodically and left even punishment to his mother. For his mother he felt a passionate demonstrative love; her large boisterous presence and her noisy charity filled the world for him; from her speech he judged her the friend of everyone, from the rector's wife to the "dear Queen", except the "Huns", the monsters who lurked in Zeppelins in the clouds. But his father's affection and dislike were as indefinite as his movements. To-night he had said he would be in Norwich, and yet you never knew. Charlie Stowe had no sense of safety as he crept down the wooden stairs. When they creaked he clenched his fingers on the collar of his nightshirt.

At the bottom of the stairs he came out quite suddenly into the little shop. It was too dark to see his way, and he did not dare touch the switch. For half a minute he sat in despair on the bottom step with his chin cupped in his hands. Then the regular movement of the searchlight was reflected through an upper window and the boy had time to fix in memory the pile of cigarettes, the counter, and the small hole under it. The footsteps of a policeman on the pavement made him grab the first packet to his hand and dive for the hole. A light shone along the floor and a hand tried the door, then the footsteps passed on, and Charlie cowered in the darkness.

At last he got his courage back by telling himself in his

adult way that if he were caught now there was nothing to be done about it, and he might as well have his smoke. He put a cigarette in his mouth and then remembered that he had no matches. For a while he dared not move. Three times the searchlight lit the shop, while he muttered taunts and encouragements. "May as well be hung for a sheep", "Cowardy, cowardy custard", grown-up and childish exhortations oddly mixed.

But as he moved he heard footfalls in the street, the sound of several men walking rapidly. Charlie Stowe was old enough to feel surprise that anybody was about. The footsteps came nearer, stopped; a key was turned in the shop door, a voice said: "Let him in," and then he heard his father, "If you wouldn't mind being quiet, gentlemen. I don't want to wake up the family." There was a note unfamiliar to Charlie in the undecided voice. A torch flashed and the electric globe burst into blue light. The boy held his breath; he wondered whether his father would hear his heart beating, and he clutched his nightshirt tightly and prayed, "O God, don't let me be caught." Through a crack in the counter he could see his father where he stood, one hand held to his high stiff collar, between two men in bowler hats and belted mackintoshes. They were strangers.

"Have a cigarette," his father said in a voice dry as a biscuit. One of the men shook his head. "It wouldn't do, not when we are on duty. Thank you all the same." He spoke gently, but without kindness: Charlie Stowe thought his father must be ill.

"Mind if I put a few in my pocket?" Mr Stowe asked, and when the man nodded he lifted a pile of Gold Flakes and Players from a shelf and caressed the packets with the tips of his fingers.

"Well," he said, "there's nothing to be done about it, and I may as well have my smokes." For a moment Charlie

Stowe feared discovery, his father stared round the shop so thoroughly; he might have been seeing it for the first time. "It's a good little business," he said, "for those that like it. The wife will sell out, I suppose. Else the neighbours'll be wrecking it. Well, you want to be off. A stitch in time. I'll get my coat."

"One of us'll come with you, if you don't mind," said the stranger gently.

"You needn't trouble. It's on the peg here. There, I'm all ready."

The other man said in an embarrassed way, "Don't you want to speak to your wife?" The thin voice was decided. "Not me. Never do to-day what you can put off till to-morrow. She'll have her chance later, won't she?"

"Yes, yes," one the strangers said and he became very cheerful and encouraging. "Don't you worry too much. While there's life . . ." and suddenly his father tried to laugh.

When the door had closed Charlie Stowe tiptoed upstairs and got into bed. He wondered why his father had left the house again so late at night and who the strangers were. Surprise and awe kept him for a little while awake. It was as if a familiar photograph had stepped from the frame to reproach him with neglect. He remembered how his father had held tight to his collar and fortified himself with proverbs, and he thought for the first time that, while his mother was boisterous and kindly, his father was very like himself, doing things in the dark which frightened him. It would have pleased him to go down to his father and tell him that he loved him, but he could hear through the window the quick steps going away. He was alone in the house with his mother, and he fell asleep.

GRAHAM GREENE

20. A SEGMENT OF GERMAN SAUSAGE

On 2 September 1940 four German agents embarked at Le Touquet in a fishing boat which was escorted across the Channel by two minesweepers. According to one of the men the fishing boat's crew consisted, improbably, of three Russians and a Latvian; another said it was manned by two Norwegians and one Russian. All had confused memories of the voyage, and it seems possible that they were drunk.

The spies were to hunt in couples. One pair, after transshipping to a dinghy, landed near Hythe in the early hours of 3 September. They had a wireless set and an elementary form of cipher, and their orders were to send back information of military importance; they had been given to understand that an invasion of the Kentish coast was imminent. By 5.30 on the same morning both men, although they separated on landing, had been challenged and made prisoner by sentries of a battalion of the Somersetshire Light Infantry.

This was hardly surprising. The two men were of Dutch nationality. They were completely untrained for their difficult task; their sole qualification for it seems to have lain in the fact that each, having committed some misdemeanour which was known to the Germans, could be blackmailed into undertaking the enterprise. Neither had more than a smattering of English, and one suffered, by virtue of having had a Japanese mother, from the additional hazard of a markedly Oriental appearance; he it was who, when first sighted by an incredulous private of the Somersets in the early dawn, had binoculars and a spare pair of shoes slung round his neck.

The other pair of spies consisted of a German, who spoke excellent French but no English at all, and a man of abstruse origins who claimed to be a Dutchman and who, alone of the four, had a fluent command of English. They landed at Dungeness under cover of darkness on 3 September, and soon after daybreak were suffering acutely from thirst, a fact which lends colour to the theory that on the previous night the whole party had relied on Dutch courage to an unwise extent. The English-speaker, pardonably ignorant of British licensing laws, tried to buy cider at breakfast-time in a public house at Lydd. The landlady pointed out that this transaction could not legally take place until ten o'clock and suggested that meanwhile he should go and look at the church. When he returned (for she was a sensible woman) he was arrested.

His companion, the only German in the party, was not caught until the following day. He had rigged up an aerial in a tree and had begun to send messages (in French) to his controllers. Copies of three of these messages survived and were used in evidence against him at his trial. They were short and from an operational point of view worthless; the news (for instance) that *"this is exact position yesterday evening six o'clock three messerschmitt fired machine guns in my direction three hundred metres south of water reservoir painted red"* was in no way calculated to facilitate the establishment of a German bridgehead in Kent.

All four spies were tried, under the Treason Act, 1940, in November. One of the blackmailed Dutchmen was acquitted; the other three men were hanged in Pentonville Prison in the following month. Their trials were conducted *in camera*, but short, factual obituary announcements were published after the executions.

Two men and a woman, who on the night of 30 September 1940 were landed by a rubber dinghy on the coast of Banff-shire after being flown thither from Norway in a seaplane, had—and, except by virtue of their courage, deserved—no more luck than the agents deposited in Kent. They were arrested within a few hours of their arrival. During those hours their conduct had been such as to attract the maximum of suspicion. This—since both men spoke English with a strong foreign accent and the documents of all three were clumsily forged—they were in no position to dispel; and the first of them to be searched by the police was found to have in his possession, *inter alia*: a wireless set; a loaded Mauser automatic; an electric torch marked "Made in Bohemia"; a list of bomber and fighter stations in East Anglia; £327 in English notes; and a segment of German sausage. Both men—one a German, the other a Swiss—were in due course hanged.

PETER FLEMING

21. THE SAD FATE OF MAJOR ANDRÉ

HE shares each want, and smiles each grief away;
And to the virtues of a noble heart,
Unites the talents of inventive art;
Since from his swift and faithful pencil flow
The lines, the camp, the fortress of the foe;
Serene to counteract each deep design,
Points the dark ambush, and the springing mine.

ANNA SEWARD

*

JOHN ANDRÉ (1751–80), major in the British army, was the son of a Genevese merchant settled in London. He received his education at Geneva, and upon his return to England became intimately connected with Miss Seward and her literary *coterie* at Lichfield, where he conceived an attachment for Honora Sneyd, subsequently the second wife of Richard Lovell Edgeworth. His relinquishment of mercantile for military pursuits has been attributed to the disappointment of his passion for this lady, whose marriage, however, did not take place till two years after the date of his commission, 4 March 1771.

He joined the British army in America, and in 1775 was taken prisoner at St John's. Upon his release he became successively aide-de-camp to General Grey and to Sir Henry Clinton, who entertained so high an opinion of him as to make him adjutant-general, notwithstanding his youth and the short period of his service. This position unhappily brought him into connection with Benedict Arnold, who was plotting the betrayal of West Point to the British. As Clinton's chief confidant, André was entrusted with the management of the correspondence with Arnold, which was disguised under colour of a mercantile transaction, Arnold signing himself Gustavus, and André adopting the name of John Anderson.

When the negotiations were sufficiently advanced (20 September 1780), André proceeded up the Hudson River in the British sloop *Vulture* to hold a personal interview with Arnold. To avoid treatment as a spy, he wore his uniform, and professed to be aiming at an arrangement with respect to the sequestrated property of Colonel Beverley Robinson, an American loyalist. His letter to Arnold on the subject having been shown by the latter to Washington, the American generalissimo so strongly protested against any interview that Arnold was compelled to resort to a secret meeting, which took place on the night of 21 September. Arnold then delivered to André full particulars respecting the defences of West Point, and concerted with him the attack which the British were to make within a few days.

Meanwhile the *Vulture* had been compelled by the fire of the American outposts to drop further down the river, and André's boatmen refused to row him back. He spent the day at the farmhouse of Joshua Smith, a tool, but probably not an accomplice, of Arnold's, and had no alternative but to disguise himself as a civilian, which, as he was within the American lines, brought him within the reach of military law as a spy. He started the following morning with a pass in the name of Anderson signed by Arnold, and under the guidance of Smith, who only left him when he seemed past all danger.

By nine on the morning of the 23rd he was actually in sight of the British lines when he was seized by three American militiamen on the look-out for stragglers. Had he produced Arnold's pass, he would have been allowed to proceed, but he unfortunately asked his captors whether they were British, and, misunderstanding their reply, disclosed his character. He was immediately searched, and the compromising papers were found in his boots. Refusing the large bribes he offered for his release, the militiamen carried him before Colonel Jameson, the commander of the outposts, who had actually sent him with the papers to Arnold, when, at the instance of Captain Talmadge, André was fetched back, and the documents forwarded to Washington. Jameson, however, reported his capture to Arnold, and the news came just in time to enable the latter to escape to the British lines.

André acknowledged his name and the character of his mission in a letter addressed to Washington on 24 September, in which he declared: "Against my stipulation, my intention, and without my knowledge beforehand, I was conducted within one of your posts." On 29 September he was brought before a military board convoked by Washington, which included Lafayette and other distinguished officers. The board found, as it could not possibly avoid finding, that André had acted in the character of a spy. He was therefore sentenced to execution by hanging. Every possible effort was ineffectually made by the British commander to save him, short of delivering up Arnold, which of course could not be contemplated. Washington has been unreasonably censured for not having granted him a more honourable death. To have done so would have implied a doubt as to the justice of his conviction.

André was executed on 2 October, meeting his fate with a

serenity which extorted the warmest admiration of the
American officers, to whom, even during the short period of
his captivity, he had greatly endeared himself. A sadder
tragedy was never enacted, but it was inevitable, and no
reproach rests upon any person concerned except Arnold.
Washington and André, indeed, deserve equal honour: André
for having accepted a terrible risk for his country and borne
the consequences of failure with unshrinking courage; and
Washington for having performed his duty to his own country
at a great sacrifice of his feelings.

RICHARD GARNETT

*

Oh WASHINGTON! I thought thee great and good,
Nor knew thy Neo-thirst of guiltless blood!
Severe to use the pow'r that fortune gave,
Thou cool determin'd murderer of the brave!
Lost to each fairer virtue, that inspires
The genuine fervour of the patriot fires!
And you, the base abettors of the doom,
That sunk his blooming honours in the tomb,
Th' opprobrious tomb your harden'd hearts decreed,
While all he ask'd was as the brave to bleed!
No other boon the glorious youth implor'd
Save the cold mercy of the warrior-sword!
O dark, and pitiless! your impious hate
O'er-whelm'd the hero in the ruffian's fate!
Stopt with the felon-cord the rosy breath!
And venom'd with disgrace the darts of death!
Remorseless WASHINGTON! the day shall come
Of deep repentance for this barb'rous doom!
When injur'd ANDRÉ's memory shall inspire
A kindling army with resistless fire;
Each falchion sharpen that the Britons wield,
And lead their fiercest lion to the field!

Then, when each hope of thine shall set in night,
When dubious dread, and unavailing flight
Impel your host, thy guilt-upbraided soul
Shall wish untouch'd the sacred life you stole!
And when thy heart appall'd, and vanquish'd pride
Shall vainly ask the mercy they deny'd,
With horror shalt thou meet the fate thou gave,
Nor pity gild the darkness of thy grave!
For infamy, with livid hand, shall shed
Eternal mildew on the ruthless head!

. . . . .

Oh murder'd ANDRÉ! for thy sacred corse;
Vain were an army's, vain its leader's sighs!—
Damp in the earth on Hudson's shore it lies!
Unshrouded welters in the wint'ry storm,
And gluts the riot of the Tappan-worm![1]

ANNA SEWARD

22. THE POLICE SPY

A SQUEAKY voice screamed, "Confession or no confession,
you are a police spy!"

The revolutionist Nikita had pushed his way in front of
Razumov, and faced him with his big, livid cheeks, his heavy
paunch, bull neck, and enormous hands. Razumov looked at
the famous slayer of gendarmes in silent disgust.

"And what are you?" he said, very low, then shut his eyes,
and rested the back of his head against the wall.

"It would be better for you to depart now." Razumov
heard a mild, sad voice, and opened his eyes. The gentle

[1] *Tappan*—The place where Major André was put to death.

speaker was an elderly man, with a great brush of fine hair making a silvery halo all round his keen, intelligent face. "Peter Ivanovitch shall be informed of your confession—and you shall be directed . . ."

Then turning to Nikita, nicknamed Necator, standing by, he appealed to him in a murmur—

"What else can we do? After this piece of sincerity he cannot be dangerous any longer."

The other muttered, "Better make sure of that before we let him go. Leave that to me. I know how to deal with such gentlemen."

He exchanged meaning glances with two or three men, who nodded slightly, then turning roughly to Razumov, "You have heard? You are not wanted here. Why don't you get out?"

The Laspara girl on guard rose, and pulled the chair out of the way unemotionally. She gave a sleepy stare to Razumov, who started, looked round the room and passed slowly by her as if struck by some sudden thought.

"I beg you to observe," he said, already on the landing, "that I had only to hold my tongue. Today, of all days since I came amongst you, I was made safe, and today I made myself free from falsehood, from remorse—independent of every single human being on this earth."

He turned his back on the room, and walked towards the stairs, but, at the violent crash of the door behind him, he looked over his shoulder and saw that Nikita, with three others, had followed him out. "They are going to kill me, after all," he thought.

Before he had time to turn round and confront them fairly, they set on him with a rush. He was driven headlong against the wall. "I wonder how," he completed his thought. Nikita cried, with a shrill laugh right in his face, "We shall make you harmless. You wait a bit."

Razumov did not struggle. The three men held him pinned against the wall, while Nikita, taking up a position a little on one side, deliberately swung off his enormous arm. Razumov, looking for a knife in his hand, saw it come at him open, unarmed, and received a tremendous blow on the side of his head over his ear. At the same time he heard a faint, dull detonating sound, as if someone had fired a pistol on the other side of the wall. A raging fury awoke in him at this outrage. The people in Laspara's rooms, holding their breath, listened to the desperate scuffling of four men all over the landing; thuds against the walls, a terrible crash against the very door, then all of them went down together with a violence which seemed to shake the whole house. Razumov, overpowered, breathless, crushed under the weight of his assailants, saw the monstrous Nikita squatting on his heels near his head, while the others held him down, kneeling on his chest, gripping his throat, lying across his legs.

"Turn his face the other way," the paunchy terrorist directed, in an excited, gleeful squeak.

Razumov could struggle no longer. He was exhausted; he had to watch passively the heavy open hand of the brute descend again in a degrading blow over his other ear. It seemed to split his head in two, and all at once the men holding him became perfectly still—soundless as shadows. In silence they pulled him brutally to his feet, rushed with him noiselessly down the staircase, and, opening the door, flung him out into the street.

He fell forward, and at once rolled over and over helplessly, going down the short slope together with the rush of running rain water. He came to rest in the roadway of the street at the bottom, lying on his back, with a great flash of lightning over his face—a vivid, silent flash of lightning which blinded him utterly. He picked himself up, and put his arm over his eyes to recover his sight. Not a sound reached him from anywhere, and he began to walk, staggering, down a long, empty street. The lightning waved and darted round him its silent flames, the water of the deluge fell, ran, leaped, drove—noiseless like the drift of mist. In this unearthly stillness his footsteps fell silent on the pavement, while a dumb wind drove him on and on, like a lost mortal in a phantom world ravaged by a soundless thunderstorm. God only knows where his noiseless feet took him to that night, here and there, and back again without pause or rest. Of one place, at least, where they did lead him, we heard afterwards; and, in the morning, the driver of the first south-shore tramcar, clanging his bell desperately, saw a bedraggled, soaked man without a hat, and walking in the roadway unsteadily with his head down, step right in front of his car, and go under.

When they picked him up, with two broken limbs and a crushed side, Razumov had not lost consciousness. It was as though he had tumbled, smashing himself, into a world of mutes. Silent men, moving unheard, lifted him up, laid him on the sidewalk, gesticulating and grimacing round him their alarm, horror, and compassion. A red face with moustaches stooped close over him, lips moving, eyes rolling. Razumov tried hard to understand the reason of this dumb show. To those who stood around him, the features of that stranger, so grievously hurt, seemed composed in meditation. Afterwards his eyes sent out at them a look of fear and closed slowly. They stared at him. Razumov made an effort to remember some French words.

"*Je suis sourd*," he had time to utter feebly, before he fainted.

"He is deaf," they exclaimed to each other. "That's why he did not hear the car . . ."

But hours before, while the thunderstorm still raged in the night, there had been in the rooms of Julius Laspara a great sensation. The terrible Nikita, coming in from the landing, uplifted his squeaky voice in horrible glee before all the company:

"Razumov! Mr Razumov! The wonderful Razumov! He shall never be any use as a spy on any one. He won't talk, because he will never hear anything in his life—not a thing! I have burst the drums of his ears for him. Oh, you may trust me. I know the trick. Ha! Ha! Ha! I know the trick."

JOSEPH CONRAD

23. SEVEN MILES FROM CALAIS

A HARSH steam siren, blasted for two full minutes as we approached the mouth of the cutting, sent to the countless workmen about me a message of release; and it being then six o'clock of the night, they came pell-mell, from the heart of the earth before us as it seemed—some crowding in the ballast-trucks, some running, some clinging to the very buffers of the little engines, some going at their ease, as though labour were not distasteful to them. That which had been a pandemonium of order and method became in a few moments a deserted scene of enterprise. None save the sentries guarded the mouth of the pit. Here and there, in the chasm below, flares began to burst up in garish yellow spirit flames; but those who worked by their light were the chosen few, the more skilled artisans, the engineers. And as we plunged downward and still downward, the great buttressed wall ever raising itself higher above us—even the skilled were rarely passed. A tremulous silence prevailed in the pit. From the distance there came a sound as of the throbbing of some mighty engine at work beneath the very sea toward which I knew we must be walking. But the man who led me downward had no desire to gratify my curiosity. Passing from the daylight to this cavernous gloom, he had become taciturn, morose, strangely self-occupied.

I followed at his heels as we went quickly ever down toward the sea. When at last the incline of the cutting ceased, and we came upon a level way, I could perceive four lines of rails running up to platforms as for the terminus of a station; and beyond them the narrow mouth of a tunnel which carried but two tracks, and seemed to be nothing else than a tube of steel thrust into the mud which here covers the chalk of the Channel bed. All the lines converged to the tunnel's mouth, but beyond was utter darkness. This was our journey's end, then.

God knows that even then I dare not ask myself the meaning of the things I saw. When, without presage, there is revealed to us, as in the twinkling of an eye, the truth of some mystery which appeals alike to the more terrible phase of our imagination and to our fear, we are slow to reckon with that truth or to admit it. I set it down that I knew from the first instant of inspection the whole meaning of that which the French contemplated against my country—there, seven miles from Calais upon the Paris road. But to claim that I realised the moment of it, or would embrace the knowledge in my innermost mind, would be to boast a prescience I have no title to. Excited if you will, driven to a curiosity which defies any measure, telling myself that I should never live again such an hour as this, I followed the man to the tunnel's mouth; I watched him kindle a flare at another a workman held; I heard his odd exclamations, that racking laugh which no other in all the world ever laughed so ill. If my life had been the stake, I must go on. Curiosity drove me now as with a lash. I neither reasoned nor apologised, for a voice within me said, You shall see.

Jeffery raised the flare and stood an instant at the very mouth of the tunnel. The waving, ugly light displayed a face hard-set as in some exciting memory. Again he looked at me as he had looked when I met him on the road to Paris.

"Sonny, ever been in a tunnel before?"

"Once, a Metropolitan tunnel."

"Nasty, eh?"

"Well, it wasn't pleasant."

"Ah, but you had the dry land above you there. You were never under the sea, I suppose?"

"Not farther than any decent swimmer goes."

"So! We'll take you deeper down than that. Come on, my boy. It does me good to hear you."

He entered the tunnel upon this and began to walk very quickly, while I, when we had left the last of the daylight behind us, stumbled after him with all a newcomer's ungainliness. Such a glare as his torch cast showed me the polished rails of steel, the circular roof above us already blackened by the smoke of engines; but the track I scarcely saw, and tripped often to his amusement.

"Miss your eyes, eh, Captain? Well, you've got to pay your footing. Listen to the music—it's a train going home to tea. You'd better step in here, my lad—we can't afford to waste your precious life like that. Do you know you're standing in what ought to be the four-foot-six, but isn't? Come out of it, come out of it."

He pulled me from the track to a manhole in the wall, and crouching there together we watched the engine go clattering by, all the roof of the tunnel incarnadined with the glowing iridescence of the crimson light, the very faces of the workmen standing out white and clear in the glow which the torch cast upward. But the tunnel seemed shaken to its very marrow, and the quivering earth, which held the steel, appeared to live while the trucks rolled over it. Again, as often before, I realised the majesty of the engineer's life; nevertheless, the greater question rang unceasingly in my ears, Why had I been seduced to this place? What did the French Government want with a tunnel beneath the sea seven miles from Calais harbour? God is my witness that I did not dare to answer myself—did not dare until many hours, nay, days were lived and I could doubt the truth no longer.

We had come by this time a mile at the least, as I judged it, from the tunnel's mouth, and must be very near to the sea, if not actually beneath it. By here and there upon our way we passed a soldier patrolling, lantern in hand, a section of the tunnel; and once, when we had gone on again a quarter of a mile, we found a great bricked shaft, at the foot of which men were hauling sleepers and steel rails by the light of a coal fire and many flares set about it. The picture was rude and wild; the faces of the men shaped pale and hard-set wherever the light fell upon them; the environing darkness, so complete, so unbroken, suggested the mouth of some vast, unfathomable pit; whereunto all this burden of steel and wood was cast; wherefrom these shadowy figures had emerged to claim a due of the outer world. But the illusion was broken when Jeffery halted to exchange rapid words with the men and to give them their directions. Again I observed the quick obedience, the respect he commanded. Of all that unnumbered army of workers I had seen he, indisputably, was General. And he knew his power.

"Clever chaps, these Frenchies," he said, as he went on again. "Direct them plainly and they'll get there, though they've a devil of a lot to say about it on the road. That shaft was an idea of mine, which I'm proud of. We'll ventilate there by-and-by; meanwhile the Belgian barges can beach their rails and send them down to us. I save two days' labour in three, and that's lucky in a job like this. Are you beginning to wonder where the coal is?"

I answered him by a question.

"Does the shaft come out on the beach, then?"

"Growing curious, eh? Well, perhaps, we'll go up by it and see as we go back. Meanwhile, you and I must have a bit of a talk for the sake of auld lang syne. Sit down, siree, sit down. The plank's not exactly Waldorf-Astoria, but it's next door to it, seeing you're in a tunnel."

We were then, I suppose, the third of a mile from the shaft he had spoken of. I knew that we were deep down below the bed of the Channel; and there was in the knowledge a sense of awe and mystery, and something beyond awe and mystery—it may be something akin to terror—which I realised then for the first time, but have lived through, waking and sleeping, many a day since that terrible hour. I was down below the sea in a tunnel that struck towards my own country. Above me were the rippling waves, the rolling ships, the flashing lights of the busiest waterway in the world. What lay beyond in the darkness, where the last tubes of this tremendous highroad were to be seen, I knew no more than the dead. The grandeur of it, the mystery of it muted my tongue, fascinated me beyond all clear thought. The road lay to England, to my home; it could not point otherwise. And I, alone of Englishmen, had come to knowledge of the mystery.

Jeffery, I say, set his flare in a crevice of the track and made a rude seat of a couple of boards and a bench which here stood in the six-foot way. Work had been progressing at this place before the siren was blown, I imagined, and the tools of the men—jacks, drills, heavy hammers—lay about as a testimony to French confusion. My guide pointed to them with an ironical finger, and, kicking a hammer from the track, made another bench similar to his own for me.

"Look," he said, "that's your Frenchman's love of order. If a ticket were needed for the Day of Judgment, he'd go aloft without it. Sit down, Hilliard, and watch me drink a sup of whisky."

He seated himself on the bench and took a long pull from

an old black flask, which he passed to me when he had done with it. My refusal to drink seemed to annoy him. It was an excuse the less for his own habit.

"Well," he snapped, "you know best. But you'll get little drink where you're going to. Here's luck on the road."

I rested my arms on my knees and looked him as full in the face as the guttering light permitted me.

"What do you mean by that, Jeffery?"

He laughed to himself, a soft, purring laugh that meant all the mischief he could command.

"Hark!" he said, raising his hand for silence; "do you hear the old girl throbbing? That's my shield—my own. There's some in Europe who would pay a penny or two if I'd make 'em another like it. But I'll wait till this job's through. Oh! sonny, wouldn't you?"

I did not answer him, but listened to the pulsing machine which, at some great distance from us, as I knew it must be, thrust its steel tongue into the soft chalk of the Channel's bed, and cast tons of the earth behind it, as though to make a burrow for a mighty, human animal which thus would cheat the seas. The tube of steel in which we had walked quivered at every thrust of the engine. Nevertheless, I knew that the work was far away; for I could hear no voices, could not even see the twinkling lamps of those who gave life to the tongue and controlled it. The very sense of distance appalled and fascinated in an appeal to the imagination surpassing any I had known.

"Jeffery," I said, asking him a plain question for the first time, "why did you bring me here?"

He answered me as plainly, "To still your d—d tongue for ever."

The words (and never a man heard seven words which meant more) were spoken in that half-mocking, half-serious key which characterised the man. To this hour I can see him squatting there upon the wooden bench, his sallow face made sardonic in the aureole of dirty light, his thin, nervous fingers interlaced, his deep-set eyes avoiding mine, but seeking, nevertheless, to watch me. And he had trapped me! My God! I tremble now when the pen recalls that hour! He had trapped me, brought me to that place because he believed that I had his secret, the secret which France had kept so well from all the world.

Fool! thrice fool I was to follow him. As one blind I had stumbled on to the mouth of the abyss; and now I could see the depths, could, in imagination, reel back from them appalled. He had trapped me!

MAX PEMBERTON

24. A TWINGE

I can never look upon the black cotton or lisle-thread gloves worn by a servant-maid without experiencing a twinge of horror.

WILLIAM LE QUEUX

Delights of the Profession

For anyone who is tired of life, the thrilling life of a spy should be the very finest recuperator.

SIR ROBERT BADEN-POWELL

25. A NARROW SQUEAK

IT was after midnight when we drove out. Conditions being favourable, it was expected that the drive over the ice to a point well along the Finnish coast—a distance of some forty miles—should take about three hours. The sleigh was of the type known as *drovny*, broad and low and filled with hay, mostly used for farm haulage. Nestling comfortably at full length under the hay I thought of long night drives in the interior in days gone by, when someone used to ride ahead on horseback with a torch to frighten away the wolves.

In a moment we were flying at breakneck speed over the ice, which was windswept after recent storms. The half-inch of frozen snow on the surface just sufficed to give grip to the horse's hoofs. Twice, bumping into snow ridges, we capsized completely. When we got going again the runners sang like a sawmill. The driver noticed this too, and was alive to the danger of being heard from shore; but his sturdy pony, exhilarated by the frosty air, was hard to restrain.

We were rapidly approaching the famous island fortress of Kronstadt. Searchlights played from time to time across the belt of ice separating the islands from the shore, to detect the smugglers who frequently used this route as we were now doing. The passage through the narrow belt was the critical point in our journey. Once past Kronstadt we should be in Finnish waters and safe.

To avoid danger from the searchlights the Finn drove within a mile of the mainland, the runners of the sleigh still hissing and singing like saws. As we entered the narrows a beam of light swept the horizon from the fortress, catching us momentarily in its track. But we were near enough to the shore to merge with its black outline.

Too near, perhaps? The dark line of the woods seemed but a stone's throw away. You could almost see the individual trees. Hell, what a noise our sleigh-runners made!

"Can't you keep the horse back a bit, man?"

"No, this is the spot we've *got* to drive past quickly."

We were crossing the line of Lissy Nos, a jutting point on the coast marking the narrowest part of the strait. Again the beam of light shot out, and the wooden pier of Lissy Nos was lit up by the flash, receding once more into darkness as we regained the open sea.

Kneeling on the heap of hay I kept my eyes riveted on the rocky promontory. We were nearly a mile away now and could no longer distinguish objects clearly.

Were those rocks—moving? I tried to pierce the darkness, my eyes rooted to the black point.

Rocks? Trees? Or—or——

I sprang up and shook the Finn by the shoulders with all my force.

"Drive like hell, man! We're being pursued!"

Riding out from Lissy Nos was a group of horsemen. My driver moaned—lashed his whip—the sleigh leapt forward—the chase began in earnest.

"Ten thousand marks if we escape!" I yelled in the Finn's ear. (It would have been a fortune to him.)

In the darkness it was impossible to tell whether we were gaining or losing. My driver uttered loud moaning cries, he seemed to be pulling very hard on the reins, the sleigh jerked so that I could hardly stand.

Then I saw that the pursuers were gaining, and gaining rapidly. The moving dots grew into galloping figures. There was a flash and a crack, then another, and another. What use was a pistol against their carbines? I threatened the driver with my revolver if he did not pull ahead, but dropped like a stone into the hay as a bullet whizzed close above.

The sleigh suddenly swung about. The driver had had difficulty with his reins, they appeared to have got caught in the shaft, and before I realised what was happening the horse fell, the sleigh whirled round and came to an abrupt stop.

What would the pursuing Red guards go for first? A fugitive? Not if there was possible loot. And what more likely than that the sleigh contained smugglers' loot?

Eel-like, I slid over the side and made in the direction of the shore. Progress was difficult, for there were big patches of windswept ice to be avoided, coal-black and slippery as glass. Stumbling along, I drew from my pocket a packet containing maps and documents which were sufficient, if discovered upon me, to assure my being shot without further ado, and held it ready to hurl away across the ice. If seized I would plead smuggling.

It seemed impossible that I should escape! Looking backward as I ran I saw the group around the sleigh. The riders, dismounted, were examining the driver. In a moment they would renew the pursuit, and I should be spotted at once. I saw already that I could never reach the shore. Yet despairingly I stumbled forward over the motley ice—grey and black in the starlight. The windswept patches looked like cavernous pits. There the surface was invisible, and incredibly slippery. *Black*—and *slippery*! Prompted by a sudden impulse, I stumbled into the middle of a broad inky patch and looked down quickly at my boots. My dark clothes made no outline. I could see no boots!

Merciful God, to have provided this! I dropped flat on the black ice and lay still. The packet I carried glided noiselessly over the inky surface to a spot where I might easily find it.

Prone, I could see neither riders nor sleigh. But the kindly ice gave warning. With my ear to its cold surface and holding my breath, I heard the sound of the approaching hoofs. Dread moment! Had I rightly understood the message that had made me fall where I was? Should I truly be unseen?

The riders did as I had done in running—they kept to the grey, they avoided the slippery black. Here they were now—close at hand—thud of hoofs muffled by crisp snow—short shouts lost on the night air. They rode so close that it seemed that one of them *must* ride over me.

Yet they didn't, after all.

An eternity of night and darkness was swallowed up while I lay motionless, until at last the riders retreated to the sleigh and rode off with it. But time is measured not by degrees of hope or despair, but by fleeting seconds and minutes, and by my luminous watch I detected that it was only half-past one. Prosaic half-past one!

Was the sombre expanse of frozen sea really deserted? Kronstadt loomed dimly on the horizon, the dark line of woods lay behind me, and all was still as death—except the imprisoned waters below, heaving in travail, groaning and gurgling as if the great ice-burden was too heavy to bear.

Slowly and imperceptibly I rose, first on all fours, then kneeling, finally standing upright. The horsemen and the sleigh were gone, I was alone. Only the stars twinkled, as much as to say: "It's all over—'twas a narrow squeak, wasn't it?—but a miss is as good as a mile!"

SIR PAUL DUKES

26. A CROSS-COUNTRY RUN

ON the evening of the 23rd May I was sitting at the window of our room, reading to my grandmother and cousin, when one of the servants rushed in, and shouted, or rather shrieked:

"Oh, Miss Belle, I t'inks de revels am a-comin', for de Yankees are a-makin' orful fuss in de street."

I immediately sprang from my seat and went to the door, and I then found that the servant's report was true. The streets were thronged with Yankee soldiers, hurrying about in every direction in the greatest confusion.

I asked a Federal officer, who just then happened to be passing by, what was the matter. He answered that the Confederates were approaching the town in force, under Generals Jackson and Ewell, that they had surprised and captured the outside pickets, and had actually advanced within a mile of the town, without the attack being even suspected.

"Now," he added, "we are endeavouring to get the ordnance and the quartermaster's stores out of their reach."

"But what will you do," I asked, "with the stores in the large dépôt?"

"Burn them, of course!"

"But suppose the rebels come upon you too quickly?"

"Then we will fight as long as we can by any possibility show a front, and in the event of defeat make good our retreat upon Winchester, burning the bridges as soon as we cross them, and finally effect a junction with General Banks' force."

I parted with the Federal officer and, returning to the house, I began to walk quietly upstairs, when suddenly I heard the report of a rifle. . . . I hurried to the balcony, and, by the aid of my glasses, descried the advance guard of the Confederates at the distance of about three-quarters of a mile, marching rapidly upon the town.

To add to my anxiety, my father, who was at that time upon General Garnett's staff, was with them. My heart beat alternately with hope and fear. I was not in ignorance of the trap the Yankees had set for my friends. I was in possession of much important information, which if I could only contrive to convey to General Jackson, I knew our victory would be secure. Without it I had every reason to anticipate defeat and disaster. . . .

I did not stop to reflect. My heart, though beating fast, was not appalled. I put on a white sun-bonnet, and started at a run down the street, which was thronged with Federal officers and men. I soon cleared the town and gained the open fields, which I traversed with unabated speed, hoping to escape observation until such time as I could make good my way to the Confederate line, which was still rapidly advancing.

I had on a dark blue dress,[1] with a little fancy white apron over it; and this contrast of colours, being visible at a great distance, made me far more conspicuous than was just then agreeable. . . .

At this moment the Federal pickets, who were rapidly falling back, perceived me still running as fast as I was able, and immediately fired upon me.

My escape was most providential; for, although I was not hit, the rifle-balls flew thick and fast about me, and more than one struck the ground so near my feet as to throw the dust in my eyes. Nor was this all: the Federals in the hospital, seeing in what direction the shots of their pickets were aimed, followed the example and also opened fire upon me.

Upon this occasion my life was spared by what seemed to me then, and seems still, little short of a miracle; for, besides the numerous bullets that whistled by my ears, several actually pierced different parts of my clothing, but not one reached my body. Besides all this, I was exposed to a cross-fire from the Federal and Confederate artillery, whose shot and shell flew whistling and hissing over my head.

At length a Federal shell struck the ground within twenty yards of my feet; and the explosion, of course, sent the frag-

[1] This dress was afterwards cut up into two shirts for two wounded Confederate soldiers.

ments flying in every direction around me. I had, however, just time to throw myself flat upon the ground before the deadly engine burst; and again Providence spared my life.

Springing up when the danger was passed, I pursued my career, still under a heavy fire. I shall never run again as I ran on that, to me, memorable day. Hope, fear, the love of life, and the determination to serve my country to the last, conspired to fill my heart with more than feminine courage, and to lend preternatural strength and swiftness to my limbs. I often marvel and even shudder when I reflect how I cleared the fields and bounded over the fences with the agility of a deer.

As I neared our line I waved my bonnet to our soldiers, to intimate that they should press forward, upon which one regiment, the 1st Maryland "rebel" Infantry, and Hay's Louisiana Brigade, gave me a loud cheer, and, without waiting for further orders, dashed upon the town at a rapid pace.

They did not then know who I was, and they were naturally surprised to see a woman on the battlefield, and on a spot, too, where the fire was so hot. Their shouts of approbation and triumph rang in my ears for many a day afterwards, and I still hear them not unfrequently in my dreams.

At this juncture the main body of the Confederates was hidden from my view by a slight elevation which intervened between me and them. My heart almost ceased to beat within me; for the dreadful thought arose in my mind that our force must be too weak to be any match for the Federals, and that the gallant men who had just been applauding me were rushing upon a certain and fruitless death. I accused myself of having urged them to their fate; and now, quite overcome by fatigue and by the feelings which tormented me, I sank upon my knees and offered a short but earnest prayer to God.

Then I felt as if my supplication was answered, and that I was inspired with fresh spirits and a new life. Not only despair, but fear also forsook me; and I had again no thought but how to fulfil the mission I had already pursued so far.

I arose from my kneeling posture, and had proceeded but a short distance, when, to my unspeakable, undescribable joy, I caught sight of the main body fast approaching; and soon an old friend and connection of mine, Major Harry Douglas, rode up, and, recognising me, cried out, while he seized my hand:

"Good God, Belle, you here! What is it?"

"Oh, Harry," I gasped out, "give me time to recover my breath."

For some seconds I could say no more; but, as soon as I had sufficiently recovered myself, I produced the "little note", and told him all, urging him to hurry on the cavalry, with orders to them to seize the bridges before the retreating Federals should have time to destroy them.

He instantly galloped off to report to General Jackson, who immediately rode forward, and asked me if I would have an escort and a horse wherewith to return to the village. I thanked him, and said, "No; I would go as I came": and then, acting upon the information I had been spared to convey, the Confederates gained a most complete victory. . . .

BELLE BOYD

27. GOOD HUNTING

NOVEMBER 23rd, 1897. One of our secret informers, the Baron de Saint-Aubanet, a former naval officer, called on me this morning in the Boulevard Malesherbes to give me an account of a very delicate mission which he has just completed in Italy.

He is a most original character. He is sixty-five years old, very alert, spick and span, very well-dressed, always has a flower in his buttonhole, has been very fond of women and is still able to please them, and adores intrigue, adventure, and nosing about. In 1891 he was pointed out, or rather handed over, to us by the Prefect of Police, Lozé, who recognised his astonishing skill in worming his way into the most varied environments and eliciting information; for the rest, he is a decent enough chap. Nisard and I always refer to him as "Casanova" or "M. de Seingalt". He was in good form today, because he had had good hunting in a certain Roman *palazzo*.

MAURICE PALÉOLOGUE

28. FOREIGN TRAVEL

BOND unfastened his seat-belt and lit a cigarette. He reached for the slim, expensive-looking attaché case on the floor beside him and took out *The Mask of Dimitrios* by Eric Ambler, and put the case, which was very heavy in spite of its size, on the seat beside him. . . .

Q Branch had put together this smart-looking little bag, ripping out the careful handiwork of Swaine and Adeney to pack fifty rounds of ·25 ammunition, in two flat rows, between the leather and the lining of the spine. In each of the innocent sides there was a flat throwing knife, built by Wilkinsons, the sword makers, and the tops of their handles were concealed cleverly by the stitching at the corners. Despite Bond's efforts to laugh them out of it, Q's craftsmen had insisted on building a hidden compartment into the handle of the case, which, by pressure at a certain point, would deliver a cyanide death-pill into the palm of his hand. . . . More important was the thick tube of Palmolive shaving cream in the otherwise guileless sponge bag. The whole top of this unscrewed to reveal the silencer for the Beretta, packed in cotton wool. In case hard cash was needed, the lid of the attaché case contained fifty golden sovereigns. These could be poured out by slipping sideways one ridge of welting.

IAN FLEMING

*

WHENEVER I was on missions abroad I was under standing orders to have an artificial tooth inserted which contained enough poison to kill me within thirty seconds if I were captured by an enemy. To make doubly sure, I wore a signet-ring in which, under a large blue stone, a gold capsule was hidden containing cyanide.

WALTER SCHELLENBERG, Head of the Foreign
Department of the German Secret Service

29. SEEX FAT ENGLISH PIGS

Scene: The private sitting-room of the Wave Crest Hotel, on the South Coast, September 1914.

Fraulein: Accident, or no accident, I like not the way that things are going. You have a telegram from Carl. What says he of tonight?

Mrs Sanderson: The troops are coming through. The emergency signal must be given.

Fraulein: At what hour?

Mrs Sanderson: It must be plainly seen at the first hour of the morning.

Fritz: De house?—it purns tonighd?

Mrs Sanderson: Yes.

Fritz: Oh, dat ees fine! Seex fat English pigs roast in deir peds!—Undt de spy—how he vill crackle!
(*He snaps his fingers illustratively.*)

Mrs Sanderson: No, no, Fritz, don't! (*She shudders and turns aside to the fireplace.*) Oh, it's too horrible! Is there no other signal we can give?

Fraulein: None. It is necessary for our safety and for the success of our plans that nobody but those to whom we send it shall ever guess the signal is a signal. It must be natural—and what more natural than that a house catch fire? It happens every day in every place. It is simple; it is sure; it is safe.

Mrs Sanderson: But, surely, there is some warning we can give the others?

Fraulein: After what has happened? It would be madness! Why should you mind? They are your enemies. And—think!—if this signal should miscarry it is the sons of the Fatherland will suffer.

Mrs Sanderson: Yes, you're quite right. The cause demands it. (*She pulls herself together and turns to* FRITZ.) Where is the petrol stored?

Fritz: In de shmall, empdy room.

Mrs Sanderson (to FRITZ): Mr Carl will give you his orders. Do nothing until you have heard from him. (*She turns to* FRAULEIN SCHROEDER.) You have packed, Luise?

Fraulein: Everything. After twenty long years of exile, I return to my own land. (*She draws her handkerchief from her belt, and dabs at her eyes.*) It is too good—too good!

Mrs Sanderson: What about your drawings?

Fraulein: They are here. (*She takes them from her bag, and gives them to* FRITZ.) I have addressed them. They are all ready. You will post them.
(FRITZ *takes the letter, slips it into his pocket, and moves up to the door.*)

Mrs Sanderson: You are sending them to London?

Fraulein: To our good friend, Mr Smith. From him they go to Holland, and from Holland to Berlin. It is so simple. (*She presses her hand to her forehead.*) I think I go now to rest until the dinner hour.

LECHMERE WORRALL and J. E. HAROLD TERRY

Room at the Bottom

"Ye have scarce the soul of a louse," he said, "but the roots of sin are there."

RUDYARD KIPLING

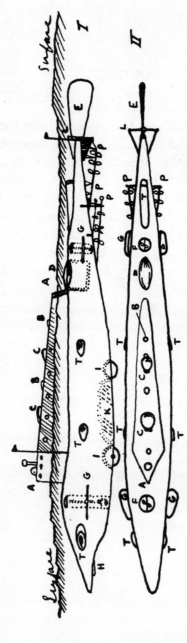

LEON KARFF'S ROUGH DRAWING OF THE NEW BRITISH SUBMARINE

The letters refer to the notes which were also found and which ran as follows: AA, Conning Tower; BB, Telephone Buoys; CC, Hatchways; D, Lifeboat (detachable); EE, Rudder; FF, Wells with Horizontal Propellers; GG, Planes; H, Hatch from Diving Chamber; II, Wheels in Recesses; K, Detachable Safety Weight in Recess; L, Tiller; TTTT, Torpedo Tubes; PPPP, Propellers.

I, Side View (in awash position).   II, Horizontal Position (from above).

Scale: ½ inch to 12 feet.

30. THE CASE OF THE DIXON TORPEDO

HEWITT was very apt in conversation to dwell upon the many curious chances and coincidences that he had observed, not only in connection with his own cases, but also in matters dealt with by the official police, with whom he was on terms of pretty regular and, indeed, friendly acquaintanceship. He has told me many an anecdote of singular happenings to Scotland Yard officials with whom he has exchanged experiences. Of Inspector Nettings, for instance, who spent many weary months in a search for a man wanted by the American Government, and in the end found, by the merest accident (a misdirected call), that the man had been lodging next door to himself the whole of the time; just as ignorant, of course, as was the inspector himself as to the enemy at the other side of the party-wall. Many criminals had met their deserts by venturing out of their own particular line of crime into another: often a man who got into trouble over something comparatively small, found himself in for a startlingly larger trouble, the result of some previous misdeed that otherwise would have gone unpunished. The rouble note-forger, Mirsky, might never have been handed over to the Russian authorities had he confined his genius to forgery alone. It was generally supposed at the time of his extradition that he had communicated with the Russian Embassy with a view to giving himself up—a foolish proceeding on his part, it would seem, since his whereabouts, indeed, even his identity as the forger, had not been suspected. He *had* communicated with the Russian Embassy, it is true, but for quite a different purpose, as Martin Hewitt well understood at the time. What that purpose was is now for the first time published.

The time was half-past one in the afternoon, and Hewitt sat in his inner office examining and comparing the handwriting of two letters by the aid of a large lens. He put down the lens and glanced at the clock on the mantelpiece with a premonition of lunch; and as he did so his clerk quietly entered the room with one of those printed slips which were kept for the announcement of unknown visitors.

It was filled up in a hasty and almost illegible hand thus:

> Name of visitor: *F. Graham Dixon*
> Address: *Chancery Lane*
> Business: *Private and urgent*

"Show Mr Dixon in," said Martin Hewitt.

Mr Dixon was a gaunt, worn-looking man of fifty or so, well although rather carelessly dressed, and carrying in his strong though drawn face and dullish eyes the look that characterises the life-long strenuous brain-worker. He leaned forward anxiously in the chair which Hewitt offered him, and told his story with a great deal of very natural agitation.

"You may possibly have heard, Mr Hewitt—I know there are rumours—of the new locomotive torpedo which the Government is thinking about adopting; it is, in fact, the Dixon torpedo, my own invention; and in every respect—not merely in my own opinion, but in that of the Government experts—by far the most efficient and certain yet produced. It will travel at least four hundred yards farther than any torpedo now made, with perfect accuracy of aim (a very great desideratum, let me tell you), and will carry an unprecedentedly heavy charge. There are other advantages—speed, simple discharge, and so forth—that I needn't bother you about. The machine is the outcome of many years of work and disappointment, and its design has only been arrived at by a careful balancing of principles and means, which are expressed on the only four existing sets of drawings. The whole thing, I need hardly tell you, is a profound secret, and you may judge of my present state of mind when I tell you that one set of drawings has been stolen."

"From your house?"

"From my office, in Chancery Lane, this morning. The four sets of drawings were distributed thus: two were at the Admiralty Office, one being a finished set on thick paper, and the other a set of tracings therefrom; and the other two were at my own office, one being a pencilled set, uncoloured—a sort of finished draft, you understand—and the other a set of tracings similar to those at the Admiralty. It is this last set that has gone. The two sets were kept together in one drawer in my room. Both were there at ten this morning, of that I am sure, for I had to go to that very drawer for something else, when I first arrived. But at twelve the tracings had vanished."

"You suspect somebody, probably?"

"I cannot. It is a most extraordinary thing. Nobody has left the office (except myself, and then only to come to you) since ten this morning, and there has been no visitor. And yet the drawings are gone!"

"But have you searched the place?"

"Of course I have. It was twelve o'clock when I first discovered my loss, and I have been turning the place upside down ever since—I and my assistants. Every drawer has been emptied, every desk and table turned over, the very carpet and linoleum have been taken up, but there is not a sign of the drawings. My men even insisted on turning all their pockets inside out, although I never for a moment suspected either of them, and it would take a pretty big pocket to hold the drawings, doubled up as small as they might be."

"You say your men—there are two, I understand—had neither left the office?"

"Neither; and they are both staying in now. Worsfold

suggested that it would be more satisfactory if they did not leave till something was done towards clearing the mystery up, and although, as I have said, I don't suspect either in the least, I acquiesced."

"Just so. Now—I am assuming that you wish me to undertake the recovery of these drawings?"

The engineer nodded hastily.

"Very good; I will go round to your office. But first perhaps you can tell me something about your assistants; something it might be awkward to tell me in their presence, you know. Mr Worsfold, for instance?"

"He is my draughtsman—a very excellent and intelligent man, a very smart man indeed, and, I feel sure, quite beyond suspicion. He has prepared many important drawings for me (he has been with me nearly ten years now), and I have always found him trustworthy. But, of course, the temptation in this case would be enormous. Still, I cannot suspect Worsfold. Indeed, how can I suspect anybody in the circumstances?"

"The other, now?"

"His name's Ritter. He is merely a tracer, not a fully skilled draughtsman. He is quite a decent young fellow, and I have had him two years. I don't consider him particularly smart, or he would have learned a little more of his business by this time. But I don't see the least reason to suspect him. As I said before, I can't reasonably suspect anybody."

"Very well; we will get to Chancery Lane now, if you please, and you can tell me more as we go."

"I have a cab waiting. What else can I tell you?"

"I understand the position to be succinctly this: the drawings were in the office when you arrived. Nobody came out, and nobody went in; and *yet* they vanished. Is that so?"

"That is so. When I say that absolutely nobody came in, of course I except the postman. He brought a couple of letters during the morning. I mean that absolutely nobody came past the barrier in the outer office—the usual thing, you know, like a counter, with a frame of ground glass over it."

"I quite understand that. But I think you said that the drawings were in a drawer in your *own* room—not the outer office, where the draughtsmen are, I presume?"

"That is the case. It is an inner room, or, rather, a room parallel with the other, and communicating with it; just as your own room is, which we have just left."

"But then you say you never left your office, and yet the drawings vanished—apparently by some unseen agency—while you were there, in the room?"

"Let me explain more clearly. I fear that I am a little confused in my explanation—I am naturally rather agitated. As you will see presently, my offices consist of three rooms, two at one side of a corridor, and the other opposite.

"In the outer office my men usually work. In the inner office I work myself. These rooms communicate by a door. Our ordinary way in and out of the place is by the door of the outer office leading into the corridor, and we first pass through the usual lifting flap in the barrier. The door leading from the *inner* office to the corridor is always kept locked on the inside, and I don't suppose I unlock it once in three months. It has not been unlocked all the morning. The drawer in which the missing drawings were kept, and in which I saw them at ten o'clock this morning, is a large chest of shallow drawers, in which the plans lie flat."

"I quite understand. Then there is the private room opposite. What of that?"

"That is a sort of private sitting-room that I rarely use, except for business interviews of a very private nature. When I said I never left my office I did not mean that I never stirred out of the inner office. I was about in one room and another, both the outer and the inner offices, and once I went into the private room for five minutes, but nobody came either in or out of any of the rooms at that time, for the door of the private room was wide open and I was standing at the bookcase (I had gone to consult a book), just inside the door, with a full view of the doors opposite. Indeed, Worsfold was at the door of the outer office most of the short time. He came to ask me a question."

"Well," Hewitt replied, "it all comes to the simple first statement. You know that nobody left the place or arrived, except the postman, who couldn't get near the drawings, and yet the drawings went. Is this your office?"

The cab had stopped before a large stone building. Mr Dixon alighted and led the way to the first floor. Hewitt took a casual glance round each of the three rooms. There was a sort of door in the frame of ground glass over the barrier, to admit of speech with visitors. This door Hewitt pushed wide open and left so.

He and the engineer went into the inner office. "Would you like to ask Worsfold and Ritter any questions?" Mr Dixon inquired.

"Presently. Those are their coats, I take it, hanging just to the right of the outer office door, over the umbrella stand?"

"Yes, those are all their things—coats, hats, stick, and umbrella."

"And those coats were searched, you say?"

"Yes."

"And this is the drawer—thoroughly searched, of course?"

"Oh, certainly, every drawer was taken out and turned over."

"Well, of course, I must assume you made no mistake in your hunt. Now tell me, did anybody know where these plans were, beyond yourself and your two men?"

"As far as I can tell, not a soul."

"You don't keep an office-boy?"

"No. There would be nothing for him to do, except to

post a letter now and again, which Ritter does quite well for."

"As you are quite sure that the drawings were there at ten o'clock, perhaps the thing scarcely matters. But I may as well know if your men have keys of the office?"

"Neither. I have patent locks to each door, and I keep all the keys myself. If Worsfold or Ritter arrive before me in the morning, they have to wait to be let in; and I am always present myself when the rooms are cleaned. I have not neglected precautions, you see."

"No. I suppose the object of the theft—assuming it is a theft—is pretty plain; the thief would offer the drawings for sale to some foreign Government?"

"Of course. They would probably command a great sum. I have been looking, as I need hardly tell you, to that invention to secure me a very large fortune, and I shall be ruined, indeed, if the design is taken abroad. I am under the strictest engagements to secrecy with the Admiralty, and not only should I lose all my labour, but I should lose all the confidence reposed in me at headquarters—should, in fact, be subject to penalties for breach of contract, and my career stopped forever. I cannot tell you what a serious business this is me. If you cannot help me, the consequences will be terrible. Bad for the service of the country, too, of course."

"Of course. Now tell me this. It would, I take it, be necessary for the thief to *exhibit* these drawings to anybody anxious to buy the secret—I mean, he couldn't describe the invention by word of mouth?"

"Oh, no, that would be impossible. The drawings are of the most complicated description, and full of figures upon which the whole thing depends. Indeed, one would have to be a skilled expert properly to appreciate the design at all. Various principles of hydrostatics, chemistry, electricity, and pneumatics are most delicately manipulated and adjusted, and the smallest error or omission in any part would upset the whole. No, the drawings are necessary to the thing, and they are gone."

At this moment the door of the outer office was heard to open, and somebody entered. The door between the two offices was ajar, and Hewitt could see right through to the glass door left open over the barrier, and into the space beyond. A well-dressed, dark, bushy-bearded man stood there carrying a hand-bag, which he placed on the ledge before him. Hewitt raised his hand to enjoin silence. The man spoke in a rather high-pitched voice and with a slight accent. "Is Mr Dixon now within?" he asked.

"He is engaged," answered one of the draughtsmen; "very particularly engaged. I'm afraid you won't be able to see him this afternoon. Can I give him any message?"

"This is two—the second time I have come to-day. Not two hours ago Mr Dixon himself tells me to call again. I have a very important—very excellent steam-packing to show him, that is very cheap and the best of the market." The man tapped his bag. "I have just taken orders from the largest railway companies. Cannot I see him, for one second only? I will not detain him."

"Really, I'm sure you can't this afternoon—he isn't seeing anybody. But if you'll leave your name——"

"My name is Hunter; but what the good of that? He ask me to call a little later and I come, and now he is engaged. It is a very great pity." And the man snatched up his bag and walking-stick and stalked off indignantly.

Hewitt stood still, gazing through the small aperture in the doorway.

"You'd scarcely expect a man with such a name as Hunter to talk with that accent, would you?" he observed musingly. "It isn't a French accent, nor a German; but it seems foreign. You don't happen to know him, I suppose?"

"No, I don't. He called here about half-past twelve, just while we were in the middle of our search, and I was frantic over the loss of the drawings. I was in the outer office myself, and told him to call later. I have lots of such agents here, anxious to sell all sorts of engineering appliances. But what will you do now? Shall you see my men?"

"I think," said Hewitt, rising, "I think I'll get you to question them yourself."

"Myself?"

"Yes, I have a reason. Will you trust me with the key of the private room opposite? I will go over there for a little, while you talk to your men in this room. Bring them in here and shut the door—I can look after the office from across the corridor, you know. Ask them each to detail his exact movements about the office this morning, and get them to recall each visitor who has been here from the beginning of the week. I'll let you know the reason of this later. Come across to me in a few minutes."

Hewitt took the key and passed through the outer office into the corridor.

Ten minutes later, Mr Dixon, having questioned his draughtsmen, followed him. He found Hewitt standing before the table in the private room, on which lay several drawings on tracing-paper.

"See here, Mr Dixon," said Hewitt; "I think these are the drawings you are anxious about?"

The engineer sprang towards them with a cry of delight. "Why, yes, yes," he exclaimed, turning them over, "every one of them. But where—how—they must have been in the place after all, then? What a fool I have been!"

Hewitt shook his head. "I'm afraid you're not quite so lucky as you think, Mr Dixon," he said. "These drawings have most certainly been out of the house for a little while. Never mind how—we'll talk of that after. There is no time to lose. Tell me, how long would it take a good draughtsman to copy them?"

"They couldn't possibly be traced over properly in less than two or two and a half long days of very hard work," Dixon replied, with eagerness.

"Ah! then, it is as I feared. These tracings have been photographed, Mr Dixon, and our task is one of every possible difficulty. If they had been copied in the ordinary way, one might hope to get hold of the copy. But photography upsets everything. Copies can be multiplied with such amazing facility that, once the thief gets a decent start, it is almost hopeless to checkmate him. The only chance is to get at the negatives before copies are taken. I must act at once; and I fear, between ourselves, it may be necessary for me to step very distinctly over the line of the law in the matter. You see, to get at those negatives may involve something very like housebreaking. There must be no delay—no waiting for legal procedure—or the mischief is done. Indeed, I very much question whether you have any legal remedy, strictly speaking."

"Mr Hewitt, I implore you, do what you can. I need not say that all I have is at your disposal. I will guarantee to hold you harmless for anything that may happen. But do, I entreat you, do everything possible. Think of what the consequences may be!"

"Well, yes, so I do," Hewitt remarked, with a smile. "The consequences to me, if I were charged with housebreaking, might be something that no amount of guarantee could mitigate. However, I will do what I can, if only from patriotic motives. Now, I must see your tracer, Ritter. He is the traitor in the camp."

"Ritter? But how?"

"Never mind that now. You are upset and agitated, and had better not know more than necessary for a little while, in case you say or do something unguarded. With Ritter I must take a deep course; what I don't know I must appear to know, and that will seem more likely to him if I disclaim acquaintance with what I do know. But first put these tracings safely away out of sight."

Dixon slipped them behind his bookcase.

"Now," Hewitt pursued, "call Mr Worsfold and give him something to do that will keep him in the inner office across the way, and tell him to send Ritter here."

Mr Dixon called his chief draughtsman and requested him to put in order the drawings in the drawers of the inner room that had been disarranged by the search, and to send Ritter, as Hewitt had suggested.

Ritter walked into the private room with an air of respectful attention. He was a puffy-faced, unhealthy-looking young man, with very small eyes and a loose, mobile mouth.

"Sit down, Mr Ritter," Hewitt said, in a stern voice. "Your recent transactions with your friend, Mr Hunter, are well known both to Mr Dixon and myself."

Ritter, who had at first leaned easily back in his chair, started forward at this, and paled.

"You are surprised, I observe; but you should be more careful in your movements out of doors if you do not wish your acquaintances to be known. Mr Hunter, I believe, has the drawings which Mr Dixon has lost, and, if so, I am certain that you have given them to him. That, you know, is theft, for which the law provides a severe penalty."

Ritter broke down completely, and turned appealingly to Mr Dixon:

"Oh, sir," he pleaded, "it isn't so bad, I assure you. I was tempted, I confess, and hid the drawings; but they are still in the office, and I can give them to you—really I can."

"Indeed!" Hewitt went on. "Then, in that case, perhaps you'd better get them at once. Just go and fetch them in—

we won't trouble to observe your hiding-place. I'll only keep this door open, to be sure you don't lose your way, you know—down the stairs, for instance."

The wretched Ritter, with hanging head, slunk into the office opposite. Presently he reappeared, looking, if possible, ghastlier than before. He looked irresolutely down the corridor, as if meditating a run for it, but Hewitt stepped towards him and motioned him back to the private room.

"You mustn't try any more of that sort of humbug," Hewitt said, with increased severity. "The drawings are gone, and you have stolen them—you know that well enough. Now attend to me. If you received your deserts, Mr Dixon would send for a policeman this moment, and have you hauled off to the gaol that is your proper place. But, unfortunately, your accomplice, who calls himself Hunter—but who has other names besides that, as I happen to know—has the drawings, and it is absolutely necessary that these should be recovered. I am afraid that it will be necessary, therefore, to come to some arrangement with this scoundrel—to square him, in fact. Now, just take that pen and paper, and write to your confederate as I dictate. You know the alternative if you cause any difficulty."

Ritter reached tremblingly for the pen.

"Address him in your usual way," Hewitt proceeded. "Say this: 'There has been an alteration in the plans.' Have you got that? 'There has been an alteration in the plans. I shall be alone here at six o'clock. Please come, without fail.' Have you got it? Very well, sign it, and address the envelope. He must come here, and then we may arrange matters. In the meantime, you will remain in the inner office opposite."

The note was written, and Martin Hewitt, without glancing at the address, thrust it into his pocket. When Ritter was safely in the inner office, however, he drew it out and read the address. "I see," he observed, "he uses the same name,

Hunter; 27 Little Carton Street, Westminster, is the address, and there I shall go at once with the note. If the man comes here, I think you had better lock him in with Ritter, and send for a policeman—it may at least frighten him. My object is, of course, to get the man away, and then, if possible, to invade his house, in some way or another, and steal or smash his negatives if they are there and to be found. Stay here, in any case, till I return. And don't forget to lock up those tracings."

It was about six o'clock when Hewitt returned, alone, but with a smiling face that told of good fortune at first sight.

"First, Mr Dixon," he said, as he dropped into an easy chair in the private room, "let me ease your mind by the information that I have been most extraordinarily lucky—in fact, I think you have no further cause for anxiety. Here are the negatives. They were not all quite dry when I—well, what?—stole them, I suppose I must say; so that they have stuck together a bit, and probably the films are damaged. But you don't mind that, I suppose?"

He laid a small parcel, wrapped in newspaper, on the table. The engineer hastily tore away the paper and took up five or six glass photographic negatives, of the half-plate size, which were damp, and stuck together by the gelatine films, in couples. He held them, one after another, up to the light of the window, and glanced through them. Then, with a great sigh of relief, he placed them on the hearth and pounded them to dust and fragments with the poker.

For a few seconds neither spoke. Then Dixon, flinging himself into a chair, said:

"Mr Hewitt, I can't express my obligation to you. What would have happened if you had failed I prefer not to think of. But what shall we do with Ritter now? The other man hasn't been here yet, by the bye."

"No—the fact is, I didn't deliver the letter. The worthy

gentleman saved me a world of trouble by taking himself out of the way." Hewitt laughed. "I'm afraid he has rather got himself into a mess by trying two kinds of theft at once, and you may not be sorry to hear that his attempt on your torpedo plans is likely to bring him a dose of penal servitude for something else. I'll tell you what has happened.

"Little Carton Street, Westminster, I found to be a seedy sort of place—one of those old streets that have seen much better days. A good many people seem to live in each house—they are fairly large houses, by the way—and there is quite a company of bell-handles on each doorpost—all down the side, like organ-stops. A barber had possession of the ground-floor front of No. 27 for trade purposes, so to him I went. 'Can you tell me,' I said, 'where in this house I can find Mr Hunter?' He looked doubtful, so I went on: 'His friend will do, you know—I can't think of his name; foreign gentleman, dark, with a bushy beard.'

"The barber understood at once. 'Oh, that's Mirsky, I expect,' he said. 'Now I come to think of it, he has had letters addressed to Hunter once or twice—I've took 'em in. Top floor back.'

"This was good, so far. I had got at 'Mr Hunter's' other alias. So, by way of possessing him with the idea that I knew all about him, I determined to ask for him as Mirsky, before handing over the letter addressed to him as Hunter. A little bluff of that sort is invaluable at the right time. At the top floor back I stopped at the door and tried to open it at once, but it was locked. I could hear somebody scuttling about within, as though carrying things about, and I knocked again. In a little while the door opened about a foot, and there stood Mr Hunter—or Mirsky, as you like—the man who, in the character of a traveller in steam-packing, came here twice to-day. He was in his shirt sleeves and cuddled something under his arm, hastily covered with a spotted pocket-handkerchief.

"'I have called to see M. Mirsky,' I said, 'with a confidential letter——'

"'Oh, yas, yas,' he answered hastily; 'I know—I know. Excuse me one minute.' And he rushed off downstairs with his parcel.

"Here was a noble chance. For a moment I thought of following him, in case there might be anything interesting in the parcel. But I had to decide in a moment, and I decided on trying the room. I slipped inside the door, and finding the key on the inside, locked it. It was a confused sort of room, with a little iron bedstead in one corner and a sort of rough boarded inclosure in another. This I rightly conjectured to be the photographic dark-room, and made for it at once.

"There was plenty of light within when the door was left open, and I made at once for the drying-rack that was fastened over the sink. There were a number of negatives in it, and I began hastily examining them one after another. In the middle of this, our friend Mirsky returned and tried the door. He rattled violently at the handle and pushed. Then he called.

"At this moment I had come upon the first of the negatives you have just smashed. The fixing and washing had evidently only lately been completed, and the negative was drying on the rack. I seized it, of course, and the others which stood by it.

"'Who are you, there, inside?' Mirsky shouted indignantly from the landing. 'Why for you go in my room like that? Open this door at once, or I call the police!'

"I took no notice. I had got the full number of negatives, one for each drawing, but I was not by any means sure that he had not taken an extra set; so I went on hunting down the rack. There were no more, so I set to work to turn out all the undeveloped plates. It was quite possible, you see, that the other set, if it existed, had not yet been developed.

"Mirsky changed his tune. After a little more banging and shouting, I could hear him kneel down and try the keyhole. I had left the key there, so that he could see nothing. But he began talking softly and rapidly through the hole in a foreign language. I did not know it in the least, but I believe it was Russian. What had led him to believe I understood Russian I could not at the time imagine, though I have a notion now. I went on ruining his stock of plates. I found several boxes, apparently of new plates, but as there was no means of telling whether they were really unused or were merely undeveloped, but with the chemical impress of your drawings on them, I dragged every one ruthlessly from its hiding-place, and laid it out in the full glare of the sunlight—destroying it thereby, of course, whether it was unused or not.

"Mirsky left off talking, and I heard him quietly sneaking off. Perhaps his conscience was not sufficiently clear to warrant an appeal to the police, but it seemed to me rather probable at the time that that was what he was going for. So I hurried on with my work. I found three dark slides—the parts that carry the plates in the back of the camera, you know —one of them fixed in the camera itself. These I opened, and exposed the plates to ruination as before. I suppose nobody ever did so much devastation in a photographic studio in ten minutes as I managed.

"I had spoilt every plate I could find and had the developed negatives safely in my pocket, when I happened to glance at a porcelain washing-well under the sink. There was one negative in that, and I took it up. It was *not* a negative of a drawing of yours, but of a Russian twenty-rouble note!

"This *was* a discovery. The only possible reason any man could have for photographing a banknote was the manufacture of an etched plate for the production of forged copies. I was almost as pleased as I had been at the discovery of *your* negatives. He might bring the police now as soon as he liked; I could turn the tables on him completely. I began to hunt about for anything else relating to this negative.

"I found an inking-roller, some old pieces of blanket (used in printing from plates), and in a corner on the floor, heaped over with newspapers and rubbish, a small copying-press. There was also a dish of acid, but not an etched plate or a printed note to be seen. I was looking at the press, with the negative in one hand and the inking-roller in the other, when I became conscious of a shadow across the window. I looked up quickly, and there was Mirsky, hanging over from some ledge or projection to the side of the window, and staring straight at me, with a look of unmistakable terror and apprehension.

"The face vanished immediately. I had to move a table to get at the window, and by the time I had opened it, there was no sign or sound of the rightful tenant of the room. I had no doubt now of his reason for carrying a parcel downstairs. He probably mistook me for another visitor he was expecting, and, knowing he must take this visitor into his room, threw the papers and rubbish over the press, and put up his plates and papers in a bundle and secreted them somewhere downstairs, lest his occupation should be observed.

"Plainly, my duty now was to communicate with the police. So, by the help of my friend the barber downstairs, a messenger was found and a note sent over to Scotland Yard. I waited, of course, for the arrival of the police, and occupied the interval in another look round—finding nothing important, however. When the official detective arrived he recognised at once the importance of the case. A large number of forged Russian notes have been put into circulation on the Continent lately, it seems, and it was suspected that they came from London. The Russian Government have been sending urgent messages to the police here on the subject.

"Of course, I said nothing about your business; but while I

was talking with the Scotland Yard man a letter was left by a messenger, addressed to Mirsky. The letter will be examined, of course, by the proper authorities, but I was not a little interested to perceive that the envelope bore the Russian Imperial arms above the words, 'Russian Embassy'. Now, why should Mirsky communicate with the Russian Embassy? Certainly not to let the officials know that he was carrying on a very extensive and lucrative business in the manufacture of spurious Russian notes. I think it is rather more than possible that he wrote—probably before he actually got your drawings—to say that he could sell information of the highest importance, and that this letter was a reply. Further, I think it quite possible that, when I asked for him by his Russian name and spoke of 'a confidential letter', he at once concluded that *I* had come from the Embassy in answer to his letter. That would account for his addressing me in Russian through the keyhole; and, of course, an official from the Russian Embassy would be the very last person in the world whom he would like to observe any indications of his little etching experiments. But anyhow, be that as it may," Hewitt concluded, "your drawings are safe now, and if once Mirsky is caught—and I think it likely, for a man in his shirt-sleeves, with scarcely any start and, perhaps, no money about him, hasn't a great chance to get away—if he is caught, I say, he will probably get something handsome at St Petersburg in the way of imprisonment, or Siberia, or what not; so that you will be amply avenged."

"Yes, but I don't at all understand this business of the drawings even now. How in the world were they taken out of the place, and how in the world did you find it out?"

"Nothing could be simpler: and yet the plan was rather ingenious. I'll tell you exactly how the thing revealed itself to me. From your original description of the case, many people would consider that an impossibility had been performed. Nobody had gone out and nobody had come in, and yet the drawings had been taken away. But an impossibility is an impossibility after all, and as drawings don't run away of themselves, plainly somebody had taken them, unaccountable as it might seem. Now, as they were in your inner office, the only people who could have got at them beside yourself were your assistants, so that it was pretty clear that one of them, at least, had something to do with the business. You told me that Worsfold was an excellent and intelligent draughtsman. Well, if such a man as that meditated treachery, he would probably be able to carry away the design in his head—at any rate, a little at a time—and would be under no necessity to run the risk of stealing a set of drawings. But Ritter, you remarked, was an inferior sort of man, 'not particularly smart', I think were your words—only a mechanical sort of tracer. *He* would be unlikely to be able to carry in his head the complicated details of such designs as yours, and, being in a subordinate position, and continually overlooked, he would find it impossible to make copies of the plans in the office. So that, to begin with, I thought I saw the most probable path to start on.

"When I looked round the rooms I pushed open the glass door of the barrier and left the door to the inner office ajar, in order to be able to see anything that *might* happen in any part of the place, without actually expecting any definite development. While we were talking, as it happened, our friend Mirsky (or Hunter—as you please) came into the outer office, and my attention was instantly called to him by the first thing he did. Did you notice anything peculiar yourself?"

"No, really I can't say I did. He seemed to behave much as any traveller or agent might."

"Well, what I noticed was the fact that as soon as he entered the place he put his walking-stick into the umbrella stand, over there by the door, close by where he stood; a most unusual

thing for a casual caller to do, before even knowing whether
you were in. This made me watch him closely. I perceived,
with increased interest, that the stick was exactly of the same
kind and pattern as one already standing there—also a curious
thing. I kept my eyes carefully on those sticks, and was all
the more interested and edified to see, when he left, that he
took the *other* stick—not the one he came with—from the
stand, and carried it away, leaving his own behind. I might
have followed him, but I decided that more could be learnt by
staying—as, in fact, proved to be the case. This, by the bye,
is the stick he carried away with him. I took the liberty of
fetching it back from Westminster, because I conceive it to
be Ritter's property."

Hewitt produced the stick. It was an ordinary thick Malacca
cane, with a buck-horn handle and a silver band. Hewitt bent
it across his knee, and laid it on the table.

"Yes," Dixon answered, "that is Ritter's stick. I think I
have often seen it in the stand. But what in the world——"

"One moment; I'll just fetch the stick Mirsky left behind."
And Hewitt stepped across the corridor.

He returned with another stick, apparently an exact facsimile of the other, and placed it by the side of the other.

"When your assistants went into the inner room, I carried
this stick off for a minute or two. I knew it was not Worsfold's, because there was an umbrella there with his initial on
the handle. Look at this."

Martin Hewitt gave the handle a twist, and rapidly unscrewed it from the top. Then it was seen that the stick was a
mere tube of very thin metal, painted to appear like a Malacca
cane.

"It was plain at once that this was no Malacca cane—it
wouldn't bend. Inside it, I found your tracings, rolled up
tightly. You can get a marvellous quantity of thin tracing-
paper into a small compass by tight rolling."

"And this—this was the way they were brought back!" the engineer exclaimed. "I see that, clearly. But how did they get away? That's as mysterious as ever."

"Not a bit of it. See here. Mirsky gets hold of Ritter, and they agree to get your drawings and photograph them. Ritter is to let his confederate have the drawings, and Mirsky is to bring them back as soon as possible, so that they shan't be missed for a moment. Ritter habitually carried his Malacca cane, and the cunning of Mirsky at once suggests that this tube should be made in outward facsimile. This morning, Mirsky keeps the actual stick and Ritter comes to the office with the tube. He seizes the first opportunity—probably when you were in this private room, and Worsfold was talking to you from the corridor—to get at the tracings, roll them up tightly, and put them in the tube, putting the tube back into the umbrella stand. At half-past twelve, or whenever it was, Mirsky turns up for the first time with the actual stick, and exchanges them, just as he afterwards did when he brought the drawings back."

"Yes, but Mirsky came half an hour after they were—oh, yes, I see. What a fool I was! I was forgetting. Of course, when I first missed the tracings they were in this walking-stick, safe enough, and I was tearing my hair out within arm's reach of them!"

"Precisely. And Mirsky took them away before your very eyes. I expect Ritter was in a rare funk when he found that the drawings were missed. He calculated, no doubt, on your not wanting them for the hour or two they would be out of the office."

"How lucky that it struck me to jot a pencil note on one of them! I might easily have made my note somewhere else, and then I should never have known that they had been away."

"Yes, they didn't give you any too much time to miss them. Well, I think the rest's pretty clear. I brought the tracings in

here, screwed up the sham stick and put it back. You identi-
fied the tracings and found none missing, and then my course
was pretty clear, though it looked difficult. I knew you would
be very naturally indignant with Ritter, so as I wanted to
manage him myself, I told you nothing of what he had
actually done, for fear that, in your agitated state, you might
burst out with something that would spoil my game. To
Ritter I pretended to know nothing of the return of the drawings or *how* they had been stolen—the only things I did know
with certainty. But I *did* pretend to know all about Mirsky—
or Hunter—when, as a matter of fact, I knew nothing at all,
except that he probably went under more than one name.
That put Ritter into my hands completely. When he found the
game was up he began with a lying confession. Believing that
the tracings were still in the stick and that we knew nothing
of their return, he said that they had not been away, and that
he would fetch them—as I had expected he would. I let him go
for them alone, and when he returned, utterly broken up by
the discovery that they were not there, I had him altogether
at my mercy. You see, if he had known that the drawings
were all the time behind your bookcase, he might have
brazened it out, sworn that the drawings had been there all
the time, and we could have done nothing with him. We
couldn't have sufficiently frightened him by a threat of prose-
cution for theft, because there the things were, in your
possession, to his knowledge.

"As it was, he answered the helm capitally: gave us
Mirsky's address on the envelope, and wrote the letter that
was to have got him out of the way while I committed bur-
glary, if that disgraceful expedient had not been rendered
unnecessary. On the whole, the case has gone very well."

"It has gone marvellously well, thanks to yourself. But
what shall I do with Ritter?"

"Here's his stick—knock him downstairs with it, if you

like. I should keep the tube, if I were you, as a memento. I don't suppose the respectable Mirsky will ever call to ask for it. But I should certainly kick Ritter out of doors—or out of window, if you like—without delay."

Mirsky was caught, and after two remands at the police-court was extradited on the charge of forging Russian notes. It came out that he had written to the Embassy, as Hewitt had surmised, stating that he had certain valuable information to offer, and the letter which Hewitt had seen delivered was an acknowledgment, and a request for more definite particulars. This was what gave rise to the impression that Mirsky had himself informed the Russian authorities of his forgeries. His real intent was very different, but was never guessed.

"I wonder," Hewitt has once or twice observed, "whether, after all, it would not have paid the Russian authorities better on the whole if I had never investigated Mirsky's little note-factory. The Dixon torpedo was worth a good many twenty-rouble notes."

ARTHUR MORRISON

31. THE ADVENTURES OF BONAPARTE

THE expulsion of the enemy consuls at Salonica [in January 1916] and the occupation of their consulates was followed by similar action in Mytilene and Corfu, and when the news about Corfu reached Athens the enemy Legations began to wonder if even they were immune from violation.

The nervousness of the personnel turned to panic when one morning H.M.S. *Folkestone*, a 496-ton armed packet-boat, dropped anchor in Phaleron Bay, for *Folkestone* was presumed to herald the arrival of the British Fleet. The Turkish Consul at the Piræus hurriedly packed a valise and fled to Athens for protection, followed by many of the Germans living at the Piræus and Phaleron. This incursion upset the nerves of the diplomatic representatives, who began to burn their archives. Smoke poured from the chimneys of the Legations all day long, and during the night what was left of the archives was distributed among various houses in Athens. One packet was sent to Mr Rhallis, the Minister for Communications. Two other packets were traced by devious ways to the German Girls' School and the Parnassus School. Three hundred thousand francs were withdrawn from the National Bank. Information reached us that von Dueffel, the assistant of the German Marine Attaché, with one of the secretaries of the Turkish Legation and a Greek courier, had been entrusted with the task of taking the archives that must be preserved to Larissa, whence they were to be sent on to Monastir. I suggested to Ricaud, my French colleague, that we should have a try at intercepting them. Ricaud was agreeable to share expenses, and we enlisted the services of five ex-brigands from Crete who, under the command of the agent Bonaparte, were to go to Larissa and there await instructions.

Twenty-three years have gone by since Bonaparte stood in the little room of those early offices at 3 Visarionos Street, but I still see him swelling with the mystery and importance of his errand, and I still hear the deep unctuous tones of his farewell:

"Skipper," he breathed hoarsely, "if they get me, you'll send my old sergeant's uniform, the one I wore at La Bassée, to my old mother in Salonique?"

"I will, Bonaparte."

He wrung my hand and moved heavily towards the door. Then he came back.

"And, Skipper, you'll tell her I died game?"

"I will, Bonaparte."

With sesquipedalian gait he plunged towards the door, only to turn back once more.

"Skipper," he asked, patting his large posterior, "do I use this?"

"Use that?" I exclaimed. "What are you going to do with that? Sit on the German bags?"

He put his hand in his hip pocket, and drew out a pistol which he looked at reverently.

"I don't want to kill anybody," he protested. "But if it's me or them, Skipper, I have your permish?"

He tapped the pistol significantly.

"You'll exercise your own discretion, Bonaparte, bearing in mind that if you make a blasted fool of yourself I shall disown you."

"Gawd bless you, Skipper, I knew I could trust you to give me a dog's chance."

With this, after once more warmly wringing me by the hand, he plunged through the door, and forth upon his secret errand.

"And a blasted fool he probably will make of himself," Tucker observed pessimistically.

"If you think that, Tucker, I'll send you instead."

"No, no, no, no," Tucker demurred hastily. "There are all these reports to get off for the Alex bag. I shall be kept pretty busy for the next few days, Captain Z."

We had given Bonaparte before he left an assumed name under which we were to communicate with him, and on the chance that the enemy might travel by train to Larissa instead of by car the railway station was watched day and night.

In the middle of all this, E. C. D. Rawlins, the British Consul at Canea in Crete, suddenly turned up from Salonica in a khaki uniform and announced that Colonel Cunliffe-Owen, the head of Army Intelligence, had told him to recruit brigands in Athens with a view to holding up the German mail after it left Sorovitch.

Rawlins was in a state of great excitement at the prospect of such an adventure, though he felt a little doubtful of the attitude the Minister might take towards such consular pranks. The idea was to dig a hole in the road and wreck the car. Sells and I sent a joint wire to Salonica, suggesting that in future some co-operation with Athens was desirable in such enterprises, because if the German mail was to be stopped on Greek territory and a serious incident provoked it would be as well to make sure beforehand that we were likely to have our money's worth. Salonica telegraphed back that nothing was going to be done there until a brigand they had dispatched to report upon the feasibleness of the scheme had returned. Next day we heard that the enemy with seven pieces of baggage had left by car for Larissa. I at once telegraphed to Bonaparte ordering him to make his dispositions to hold up the car and avoid if possible any loss of life. I instructed him to escape after the attempt across country to Caterina Point, take a caïque thence to Salonica, and deliver the papers to Lieut.-Colonel Cunliffe-Owen at A.H.Q. At the same time Sells warned the naval authorities of his possible arrival so that there should be no delay through the action of our patrols.

The next day after this, three of the brigands we had sent with Bonaparte returned to Athens, having been compelled to leave Larissa by the local police. I asked them what Bonaparte had been doing all this while, and they told us that they had not caught a glimpse of him. I then telegraphed again urgently to Bonaparte under his assumed name, but received no reply. We could only conclude that he had been arrested and wondered what was the prudent way to get him released. It happened that George Leith came in while we were discussing the best steps to take, and he at once volunteered to go up to Larissa himself, and find out what was happening there. This was a capital solution of the problem, for as a member of the British Naval Mission with the rank of Captain in the

Greek Navy he was not likely to be troubled by the attentions of the police. George Leith went first to the post office and found that the two telegrams addressed there to Bonaparte under his assumed name had not been called for. He then went to the chief hotel, and while he was in the lavatory washing his hands he heard from inside one of the cabinets a low voice hoarse with apprehension calling to him:

"Captain Georgie, Captain Georgie! It's me, it's Bonaparte. Can you get me out of here, Captain Georgie? I've had to sit in here for all the last two days, Captain Georgie."

"Well, I've got a bottle of stoppers with me, so come out," said George Leith, "and I'll dose you."

"It's not my stomach, Captain Georgie," Bonaparte breathed from the other side of the door. "It's the police. As soon as I got out of the train at Larissa they started following me around. Then I forgot the name Captain Z gave me, and I didn't dare ask at the post office if there was any telegrams in case they run me in, and oh, my gawd, Captain Georgie, I'm glad you've come. I've had a cruel time, sitting in here for two days and not daring to put my nose outside for fear of being arrested by these Greeks."

Presently under encouragement from George Leith, Bonaparte emerged. Having been reminded of his name, he amassed enough courage to go and fetch his telegrams, after which he got into touch with the two other brigands. Finding that the mail would not leave Larissa until two mornings later he returned with George Leith to Athens and reported to me.

"A nice mess you've made of the first important mission I give you," I said angrily.

Bonaparte held up one large fleshy paw and with the other mopped his forehead with a musk-scented handkerchief.

"Skipper, there was too many for me. Larissa was stinking with police."

"You're nothing but a damned coward," I told him.

"Skipper, that don't come nice from you. Bonaparte is afraid of nothing and nobody within reason. I'm only a sergeant, but I know my duty. Don't say things you'll regret afterwards, Skipper. What could I do locked up for two days in a lavatory? They kept coming and trying the door until I shouted out, 'The next B who tries this B door I'll plug him.' And so I would have, Captain Z. I had a pistol on the seat each side of me. I meant to die fighting. That's Bonaparte. Game to the last, Skipper."

"You great buffoon, you were so frightened that you even forgot the name I'd given you."

"Now, Skipper, that's not a fair thing to say. Nobody can answer for his memory all the time, and that's how I first come into the lavatory. I wanted somewhere I could think quiet what name you give me. I've done the best I could, Skipper."

COMPTON MACKENZIE

Unexpected Encounters

Thrust in one pew
By chance that day . . .

THOMAS HARDY

32. COLETTE AND MATA HARI

FROM behind a screen of foliage a naked woman had appeared, riding on a white horse, its strappings studded with turquoises—a new dancer whose name was already known among the studio and drawing-room cliques: Mata Hari.

She was a dancer who did not dance much, yet at Emma Calve's, before the portable altar that she used as a background, supported by a little group of coloured attendants and musicians and framed in the pillars of a vast, white hall, she had been sufficiently snake-like and enigmatic to produce a good effect. The people who fell into such dithyrambic raptures and wrote so enthusiastically of Mata Hari's person and talents must be wondering now what collective delusion possessed them. Her dancing and the naïve legends surrounding her were of no better quality than the ordinary claptrap of the current 'Indian turns' in the music hall. The only pleasant certainties on which her drawing-room audiences could count were a slender waist below breasts that she prudently kept hidden, a fine, supple moving back, muscular loins, long thighs and slim knees. Her nose and mouth, which were both thick, and the rather oily brilliance of her eyes did nothing to alter—on the contrary—our established notions of the Oriental. It should be said that the finale of her dance, the moment when Mata Hari, freed of her last girdle, fell forward modestly upon her belly, carried the male —and a good proportion of the female—spectators to the extreme limit of decent attention.

In the May sunshine, at Neuilly, despite the turquoises,

the dropping black mane of hair, the tinsel diadem and especially the long thigh against the white flanks of her Arab horse, the colour of her skin was disconcerting, no longer brown and luscious as it had been by artificial light but a dubious, uneven purple. Having finished her equestrian parade, she alighted and wrapped herself in a sari. She bowed, talked, was faintly disappointing. It was much worse on the day Miss Barney invited her as an ordinary guest to a second garden-party.

"Madame Colette Willy?"

A loud, strongly-stressed voice, calling me by my fancy name, made me turn round. I found a lady in a black and white check suit, her breasts held high by a boned cuirass of stays, a veil with velvet chenille dots upon her nose, holding out a hand tightly gloved in white glacé kid stitched with black. I also remember a frilled shirt with a stiff collar and a pair of shoes of a bright egg colour. I remember my amazement.

The lady laughed heartily, displaying a set of strong, white teeth, gave me her name, wrung my hand, expressed the hope that we might meet again and did not move a muscle as the voice of Lady W—— rose beside us, saying in clear, plain words:

"She an Oriental? Don't be silly! Hamburg or Rotterdam, or possibly Berlin."

COLETTE

33. THE MAN IN THE SOFT CAP

On the evening of September 2 [1915], the battalion moved cautiously from Mailly-Maillet by cross-country tracks, through pretty Englebelmer, with ghostly Angelus on the green and dewy light, over the downs to Mesnil, and assembled in the Hamel trenches to attack the Beaucourt ridge next morning. The night all round was drowsily quiet. I stood at the junction of four forward trenches, directing the several companies into them as had been planned. . . . The cold disturbing air and the scent of the river mist marked the approach of the morning. I got my fellow-officer to move his men nearer to my main supply of bombs, which were ready in canvas buckets; and time slipped by, until scarcely five preliminary minutes remained. . . . As for me, I took off my equipment and began to set out the bomb buckets in a side trench so that the carriers could at the right moment pick them up two at a time; and while I was doing this, and the east began to unveil, a stranger in a soft cap and a trench coat approached, and asked me the way to the German lines. This visitor was white-faced as a ghost, and I liked neither his soft cap nor the mackintosh nor the right hand concealed under his coat. I, too, felt myself grow pale, and I thought it as well to show him the communication trench, Devial Alley, then deserted; he scanned me, and quickly went on. Who he was, I have never explained to myself; but in two minutes the barrage opened, and his chances of doing us harm (I thought he must be a spy) were all gone.

EDMUND BLUNDEN

34. A MEET IN THE SHIRES

THE morning was one of those damp cold ones of mid-February; the frost had given and everyone expected a good run, for the scent would be excellent. Riding side by side with my fair companion, we chatted and laughed as we went along, until, on reaching the cover, we drew up with the others and halted while hounds went in.

The first cover was, however, drawn blank, but from the second a fox went away straight for Elton, and soon the hounds were in full cry after him and we followed at a gallop. After a couple of miles more than half the field were left behind, still we kept on, until of a sudden, and without effort, my companion took a high hedge and was cutting across the pastures ere I knew that she had left the road. That she was a straight rider I at once saw, and I must confess that I preferred the gate to the hedge and ditch which she had taken so easily.

Half an hour later the kill took place near Haddon Hall, and of the half-dozen in at the death Beatrice Graham was one.

When I rode up, five minutes afterwards, she smiled at me. Her face was a trifle flushed by hard riding, yet her hair was in no way awry, and she declared that she had thoroughly enjoyed that tearing gallop.

Just, however, as we sat watching Barnard cut off the brush, a tall, rather good-looking man rode up, having apparently been left just as I had. As he approached I noticed that he gave my pretty friend a strange look, almost as of warning, while she on her part, refrained from acknowledging him. It was as though he had made her some secret sign which she had understood.

But there was a further fact that puzzled me greatly.

I had recognised in that well-turned-out hunting man someone whom I had had distinct occasion to recollect. At first I failed to recall the man's identity, but when I did, a few moments later, I sat regarding his retreating figure like one in a dream. The horseman who rode with such military bearing was none other than the renowned spy, one of the cleverest secret agents in the world, Otto Krempelstein, Chief of the German Secret Service.

WILLIAM LE QUEUX

Not Known to the Secret Services

And many more Destructions played
In this ghastly masquerade,
All disguised, even to the eyes,
Like Bishops, lawyers, peers, or spies.

PERCY BYSSHE SHELLEY

35. THE SPIES' MARCH, 1913

("The outbreak is in full swing and our death-rate would sicken Napoleon. . . . Dr M— died last week, and C— on Monday, but some more medicines are coming. . . . We don't seem to be able to check it at all. . . . Villages panicking badly. . . . In some places not a living soul. . . . But at any rate the experience gained may come in useful, so I am keeping my notes written up to date in case of accidents. . . . Death is a queer chap to live with for steady company."—*Extract from a private letter from Manchuria.*)

THERE are no leaders to lead us to honour, and yet without
      leaders we sally;
Each man reporting for duty alone, out of sight, out of reach,
      of his fellow.
There are no bugles to call the battalions, and yet without
      bugle we rally
From the ends of the earth to the ends of the earth, to follow
      the Standard of Yellow!
      Fall in! O fall in! O fall in!

Not where the squadrons mass,
    Not where the bayonets shine,
Not where the big shells shout as they pass
    Over the firing-line;
Not where the wounded are,
    Not where the nations die,
Killed in the cleanly game of war—
    That is no place for a spy!
O Princes, Thrones and Powers, your work is less than ours—
    Here is no place for a spy!

131

Trained to another use,
　　We march with colours furled,
Only concerned when Death breaks loose
　　On a front of half a world,
Only for General Death
　　The Yellow Flag may fly,
While we take post beneath—
　　That is the place for a spy
Where Plague has spread his pinions over Nations and
　　　　Dominions—
　　Then will be work for a spy!

The dropping shots begin,
　　The single funerals pass,
Our skirmishers run in,
　　The corpses dot the grass!
The howling towns stampede,
　　The tainted hamlets die.
Now it is war indeed—
　　Now there is room for a spy!
O Peoples, Kings and Lands, we are waiting for your
　　　　commands—
　　What is the work for a spy?
　　　　　(Drums)—*Fear is upon us, spy!*

"Go where his pickets hide—
　　Unmask the shape they take,
Whether a gnat from the waterside,
　　Or a stinging fly in the brake,
Or filth of the crowded street,
　　Or a sick rat limping by,
Or a smear of spittle dried in the heat—
　　That is the work for a spy!
　　　　　(Drums)—*Death is upon us, spy!*

"What does he next prepare?
  Whence will he move to attack?
By water, earth or air?—
  How can we head him back?
Shall we starve him out if we burn
  Or bury his food-supply?
Slip through his lines and learn—
  That is the work for a spy!
        (Drums)—*Get to your business, spy!*

"Does he feint or strike in force?
  Will he charge or ambuscade?
What is it checks his course?
  Is he beaten or only delayed?
How long will the lull endure?
  Is he retreating? Why?
Crawl to his camp and make sure—
  That is the work for a spy!
        (Drums)—*Fetch us our answer, spy!*

"Ride with him girth to girth
  Wherever the Pale Horse wheels.
Wait on his councils, ear to earth,
  And show what the dust reveals.
For the smoke of our torment rolls
  Where the burning corpses lie;
What do we care for men's bodies or souls?
  Bring us deliverance, spy!"

                              RUDYARD KIPLING

36. A ROYAL SPY

I

PRINCE and Princess Oscar received their distinguished guests with a show of pleasure that did credit to their powers of dissimulation. . . . That the *raison d'être* of the visit was not for a moment to be lost sight of was made plain when, after dinner, the Chancellor and chief officers retired into the selected apartment for the first discussion of the subject that had necessitated the meeting. And with them went Prince Oscar.

From that time on, for three or four days, the young Prince became more and more reserved in his manner, and the Princess, quick in perception, taxed him with holding some unwholesome secret and pressed him to make her his confidante. Alas! he could but reply that such things as his father's representatives and he discussed in private were not for women's ears; but her loving heart guessed well that the matter touched her more nearly, as an Englishwoman, than they would have cared to confess.

One day, as she was passing the door of the conference chamber, it was flung open and a naval captain, acting as secretary, came out. Through the open door a loud voice, raised in anger, sounded:

". . . not to give England any warning? I call it . . ." and the door closed again, shutting from her ears the closing words of her husband; for she had recognised his voice, speaking in evident protest—against what or whom she could only guess.

From that hour she ceased worrying her husband, knowing full well that his honour depended on the maintenance of silence as regards the secret locked in his breast.

But one idea possessed her soul to the exclusion of all other thoughts—she must warn England, her England, that danger, some inconceivable, awful danger, threatened the British Empire.

All that was English in her rose up in revolt against the treachery she could not but impute to the Imperial Chancellor, and though desirous of avoiding any active part in international politics, recognising the folly of such interference from one in her position, the thought that her native land might be devastated by the underhand designs and specious cunning of her adopted country, made it essential that she should in some way warn it of its danger.

Calmer consideration caused her to realise how slight was the evidence upon which she based her fears. She herself might feel convinced that treachery was intended,—but would hard-headed, commonsense Englishmen credit it? Impossible—she felt it to be impossible—but beneath this feeling lay that subtle womanly instinct which spelt danger clearer than written words.

She would try to learn more!

She, a Princess of Royal Blood, to spy? For a moment the very idea stupefied her, appalled her inborn sense of honour. Yet, were they honourable in their designs? Surely if they were plotting to bring about the downfall of her dear nativeland, she would be justified in the use of any means whatsoever to circumvent them. . . .

II

There was more than the usual excitement amongst the passengers aboard the Belgian packet *Marie Henriette* as she sped at nearly twenty-two knots across the Channel on the morning of June 7th,—as bright a Monday as had ever initiated a fresh week. Princess Alexandra was with them, on her first visit to England since her marriage, and locked in her bosom lay the most terrible secret ever held by woman.

Outwardly calm, she rated the speed of the vessel as sluggish and looked anxiously ahead at the rising land, longing with an inexpressible longing to be once more on English soil,—and, above all things, to see her august uncle and un-burden herself to him, for to him alone would she speak.

Little she attended the unctuous reception by an adoring people, little she noticed the fulsome compliments of the local Mayor who, berobed and chained, offered her a hearty welcome in the nation's name. She was all for pushing on and had no relief even when, on the arrival of her train in London, her mother held her clasped tightly and lovingly to her breast.

"My darling child, thank Heaven for this great joy! Tell me, how has it been with you since you left; how is dear Oscar, and why this hasty decision to visit us?"

"Mother, oh, Mother! Take me to my uncle the King,—do, do—if you love me, take me to him!" were her answering words, and her astonished mother stood back aghast, wondering whether anything could have unhinged the fresh young mind.

"But, Xandra, you cannot mean it! He is presiding at a banquet at Buckingham Palace and to have an immediate audience of him is quite out of the question. Compose yourself, my daughter, and tell me of your trouble."

"Don't put me off, mother," she cried imploringly. "It is a matter for the King's ear only. Oh! Major Vere," she continued, turning to an equerry, "cannot you see I am in earnest? Believe me, the safety of England depends upon it and I dare not tell my secret to any but the King."

And so strongly did she plead and so sanely, that at last a motor was ordered and she and her mother driven off to the Palace.

But the Goddess of Chance was fighting against England that day.

Down the great length of Pall Mall dashed the car, sharply spinning round past Marlborough House,—then away on the last short stretch towards the Palace. When not forty yards remained to be covered, a loud report rang out and the motor swerved giddily to the left and collided with great violence with an electric arc-standard.

A tyre had burst and taken the chauffeur utterly by surprise.

From all sides people came to render aid and willing hands lifted a fair young form tenderly from the ground and bore it gently to the Palace. The Duchess was merely badly shaken and walked, as in a dream, after her senseless daughter, leaving the injured chauffeur to the good services of the police....

Placed on a downy bed, amid surroundings of the greatest luxury lay the sole means of warning England of such danger as she had never, until then, been called upon to face.

Hurried messengers had motored hot-haste to the Court Physicians and soon three kindly faced men stood in consultation over the girl's apparently inanimate body....

For long hours they watched thus and as each hour chimed from some near spire the anxiety deepened on the set face of the doctor, who kept a lonely vigil, holding his patient's hand between his own.... Into the early hours of the next morning he watched and watched, and prayed too, but never a sign was vouchsafed him. At last, when hope had sunk to zero and he had almost given way to despair, a slight, almost inaudible sigh from the bed sent the blood tingling through his veins. He touched a button at his side and a muffled bell clicked once; a uniformed nurse crept in and approached him, and after a whispered word or two left the room as softly as she had entered.

Ten minutes elapsed and the door again opened. The Duchess entered, clad in a hastily donned tea-gown; behind her strode a fine, manly figure, bearded of feature yet regal in bearing and carriage. The doctor leapt instantly to his feet.

It was His Majesty the King!

"Well, Sir Arthur, how is our little patient progressing?" he whispered, as the great specialist moved to meet him.

"She is coming round fast, your Majesty, and as she had, I am told, been asking for you immediately prior to the accident, it is not unlikely the line of thought will follow in direct sequence and her first desire will be for you, sire. Therefore I dared to have you roused, and crave your forgiveness if I have done wrong."

"Indeed I expected to be sent for, Sir Arthur, but appreciate your thoughtfulness nevertheless. Sh-h-h, my little niece is coming round. See—her eyes are open."

The doctor returned to the bedside where the nurse was ministering to the girl, now momentarily recovering from the effects of the accident. He held a spoonful of weak spirit to her lips, and as she swallowed it a happy smile spread over her wan features.

Then she espied the King and made an obvious effort to speak to him.

"Not yet, dearie, not yet," said her mother soothingly. "Wait until tomorrow and you shall tell us everything."

But the Princess essayed to speak.

"The Germans," she began weakly, half rising in spite of all remonstrances. "Oh, uncle,—the—the—Germans—sending—torpedo boats—to—to" here her strength failed her and she fell back with a heavy sigh and lapsed into unconsciousness.

But it was not to Princess Oscar that the other occupants of the room turned,—it was to King Edward.

Her whispered words, enigmatical to the rest, burned deep into his very soul. He clutched Sir Arthur by the shoulder and repeating what the Princess had said inquired hoarsely:

"Did she say that? Did she say that?"

A sudden fear had gripped him, and his heart became heavy as stone. He guessed intuitively what his niece had wished to convey and grew cold with horror as he thought of nearly his entire navy strung out at Spithead, an easy prey to a determined and vengeful foe.

ALAN H. BURGOYNE

37. SCHNITZEL ALIAS JONES

My going to Valencia was entirely an accident. But the more often I stated that fact, the more satisfied was everyone at the capital that I had come on some secret mission. Even the venerable politician who acted as our minister, the night of my arrival, after dinner, said confidentially, "Now, Mr Crosby, between ourselves, what's the game?"

"What's the game?" I asked.

"You know what I mean," he returned. "What are you here for?"

But when, for the tenth time, I repeated how I came to be marooned in Valencia he showed that his feelings were hurt, and said stiffly: "As you please. Suppose we join the ladies."

And the next day his wife reproached me with: "I should think you could trust your own minister. My husband *never* talks—not even to me."

"So I see," I said.

And then her feelings were hurt also, and she went about telling people I was an agent of the Walker-Keefe crowd.

My only reason for repeating here that my going to Valencia was an accident is that it was because Schnitzel disbelieved that fact, and to drag the hideous facts from me followed me back to New York. Through that circumstance I came to know him, and am able to tell his story.

The simple truth was that I had been sent by the State Department to Panama to "go, look, see", and straighten out a certain conflict of authority among the officials of the canal zone. While I was there the yellow-fever broke out, and every self-respecting power clapped a quarantine on the Isthmus, with the result that when I tried to return to New York no steamer would take me to any place to which any white man would care to go. But I knew that at Valencia there was a direct line to New York, so I took a tramp steamer down the coast to Valencia. I went to Valencia only because to me every other port in the world was closed. My position was that of the man who explained to his wife that he came home because the other places were shut.

But, because formerly in Valencia I had held a minor post in our legation, and because the State Department so constantly consults our firm on questions of international law, it was believed I revisited Valencia on some mysterious and secret mission.

As a matter of fact, had I gone there to sell phonographs or to start a steam laundry, I should have been as greatly suspected. For in Valencia even every commercial salesman, from the moment he gives up his passport on the steamer until the police permit him to depart, is suspected, shadowed, and begirt with spies.

I believe that during my brief visit I enjoyed the distinction of occupying the undivided attention of three: a common or garden Government spy, from whom no guilty man escapes, a Walker-Keefe spy, and the spy of the Nitrate Company. The spy of the Nitrate Company is generally a man you meet at the legations and clubs. He plays bridge and is dignified with the title of "agent". The Walker-Keefe spy is ostensibly a travelling salesman or hotel runner. The Government spy is just a spy—a scowling, important little beast in a white duck suit and a diamond ring. The limit of his intelligence is to follow you into a cigar store and note what cigar you buy, and in what kind of money you pay for it.

The reason for it all was the three-cornered fight which then was being waged by the Government, the Nitrate Trust, and the Walker-Keefe crowd for the possession of the nitrate beds. Valencia is so near to the equator, and so far from New York, that there are few who studied the intricate story of that disgraceful struggle, which, I hasten to add, with the fear of libel before my eyes, I do not intend to tell now.

Briefly, it was a triangular fight between opponents each of whom was in the wrong, and each of whom, to gain his end, bribed, blackmailed, and robbed, not only his adversaries, but those of his own side, the end in view being the possession of those great deposits that lie in the rocks of Valencia, baked from above by the tropic sun and from below by volcanic fires. As one of their engineers, one night in the Plaza, said to me: "Those mines were conceived in hell, and stink to heaven, and the reputation of every man of us that has touched them smells like the mines."

At the time I was there the situation was "acute". In Valencia the situation always is acute, but this time it looked as though something might happen. On the day before I departed the Nitrate Trust had cabled vehemently for warships, the Minister of Foreign Affairs had refused to receive our minister, and at Porto Banos a mob had made the tin sign of the United States consulate look like a sieve. Our minister urged me to remain. To be bombarded by one's own warships, he assured me, would be a thrilling experience.

But I repeated that my business was with Panama, not Valencia, and that if in this matter of his row I had any weight at Washington, as between preserving the nitrate beds for the trust, and preserving for his country and various sweethearts one brown-throated, clean-limbed bluejacket, I was for the bluejacket.

Accordingly, when I sailed from Valencia the aged diplomat would have described our relations as strained.

Our ship was a slow ship, listed to touch at many ports, and as early as noon on the following day we stopped for cargo at Trujillo. It was there I met Schnitzel.

In Panama I had bought a macaw for a little niece of mine, and while we were taking on cargo I went ashore to get a tin cage in which to put it, and, for direction, called upon our consul. From an inner room he entered excitedly, smiling at my card, and asked how he might serve me. I told him I had a parrot below decks, and wanted to buy a tin cage.

"Exactly. You want a tin cage," the consul repeated soothingly. "The State Department doesn't keep me awake nights cabling me what it's going to do," he said, "but at least I know it doesn't send a thousand-dollar-a-minute, four-cylinder lawyer all the way to this fever swamp to buy a tin cage. Now, honest, how can I serve you?" I saw it was hopeless. No one would believe the truth. To offer it to this friendly soul would merely offend his feelings and his intelligence.

So, with much mystery, I asked him to describe the "situation", and he did so with the exactness of one who believes that within an hour every word he speaks will be cabled to the White House.

When I was leaving he said: "Oh, there's a newspaper correspondent after you. He wants an interview, I guess. He followed you last night from the capital by train. You want to watch out he don't catch you. His name is Jones." I promised to be on my guard against a man named Jones, and the consul escorted me to the ship. As he went down the accommodation ladder, I called over the rail: "In case they *should* declare war, cable to Curaçao, and I'll come back. And don't cable anything indefinite, like 'Situation critical' or 'War imminent'. Understand? Cable me, 'Come back' or 'Go ahead'. But whatever you cable, make it *clear*."

He shook his head violently and with his green-lined umbrella pointed at my elbow. I turned and found a young man hungrily listening to my words. He was leaning on the rail with his chin on his arms and the brim of his Panama hat drawn down to conceal his eyes.

On the pier-head, from which we now were drawing rapidly away, the consul made a megaphone of his hands.

"That's *him*," he called. "That's Jones."

Jones raised his head, and I saw that the tropical heat had made Jones thirsty, or that with friends he had been celebrating his departure. He winked at me, and, apparently with pleasure at his own discernment and with pity for me, smiled.

"Oh, of course!" he murmured. His tone was one of heavy irony. "Make it 'clear'. Make it clear to the whole wharf. Shout it out so's everybody can hear you. You're 'clear' enough." His disgust was too keen for ordinary words. "My uncle!" he exclaimed.

By this I gathered that he was expressing his contempt.

"I beg your pardon?" I said.

We had the deck to ourselves. Its emptiness suddenly reminded me that we had the ship, also, to ourselves. I remembered the purser had told me that, except for those who travelled overnight from port to port, I was his only passenger.

With dismay I pictured myself for ten days adrift on the high seas—alone with Jones.

With a dramatic gesture, as one would say, "I am here!" he pushed back his Panama hat. With an unsteady finger he pointed, as it was drawn dripping across the deck, at the stern hawser.

"You see that rope?" he demanded. "Soon as that rope hit the water I knocked off work. S'long as you was in Valencia—me, on the job. Now, *you* can't go back, *I* can't go back. Why further dissim'lation? *Who am I?*"

His condition seemed to preclude the possibility of his knowing who he was, so I told him.

He sneered as I have seen men sneer only in melodrama.

"Oh, of course," he muttered. "Oh, of course."

He lurched towards me indignantly.

"You know perfec'ly well Jones is not my name. You know perfec'ly well who I am."

"My dear sir," I said, "I don't know anything about you, except that you're a damned nuisance."

He swayed from me, pained and surprised. Apparently he was upon an outbreak of tears.

"Proud," he murmured, "*and* haughty. Proud and haughty to the last."

I never have understood why an intoxicated man feels the climax of insult is to hurl at you your name. Perhaps because he knows it is the one charge you cannot deny. But invariably before you escape, as though assured the words will cover your retreat with shame, he throws at you your full title. Jones did this.

Slowly and mercilessly he repeated, "Mr—George—Morgan—Crosby. Of Harvard," he added. "Proud and haughty to the last."

He then embraced a passing steward, and demanded to be informed why the ship rolled. He never knew a ship to roll as our ship rolled.

"Perfec'ly satisfact'ry ocean, but ship—rolling like a stone-breaker. Take me some place in the ship where this ship don't roll."

The steward led him away.

When he had dropped the local pilot the captain beckoned me to the bridge.

"I saw you talking to Mr Schnitzel," he said. "He's a little under the weather. He has too light a head for liquors."

I agreed that he had a light head, and said I understood his name was Jones.

"That's what I wanted to tell you," said the captain. "His

name is Schnitzel. He used to work for the Nitrate Trust in New York. Then he came down here as an agent. He's a good boy not to tell things to. Understand? Sometimes I carry him under one name, and the next voyage under another. The purser and he fix it up between 'em. It pleases him, and it don't hurt anybody else, so long as I tell them about it. I don't know who he's working for now," he went on, "but I know he's not with the Nitrate Company any more. He sold them out."

"How could he?" I asked. "He's only a boy."

"He had a berth as typewriter to Senator Burnsides, president of the Nitrate Trust, sort of confidential stenographer," said the captain. "Whenever the senator dictated an important letter, they say, Schnitzel used to make a carbon copy, and when he had enough of them he sold them to the Walker-Keefe crowd. Then, when Walker-Keefe lost their suit in the Valencia Supreme Court I guess Schnitzel went over to President Alvarez. And again, some folks say he's back with the Nitrate Company."

"After he sold them out?"

"Yes, but you see he's worth more to them now. He knows all the Walker-Keefe secrets and Alvarez's secrets, too."

I expressed my opinion of every one concerned.

"It shouldn't surprise *you*," complained the captain. "You know the country. Every man in it is out for something that isn't his. The pilot wants his bit, the health doctor must get his, the customs take all your cigars, and if you don't put up gold for the captain of the port and the *alcalde* and the commandant and the harbour police and the foreman of the *cargadores*, they won't move a lighter, and they'll hold up the ship's papers. Well, an American comes down here, honest and straight and willing to work for his wages. But pretty quick he finds every one is getting his squeeze but him, so he tries to get some of it back by robbing the natives that robbed

him. Then he robs the other foreigners, and it ain't long
before he's cheating the people at home who sent him here.
There isn't a man in this nitrate row that isn't robbing the
crowd he's with, and that wouldn't change sides for money.
Schnitzel's no worse than the president nor the canteen contractor."

He waved his hand at the glaring coastline, at the steaming
swamps and the hot, naked mountains.

"It's the country that does it," he said. "It's in the air. You
can smell it as soon as you drop anchor, like you smell the
slaughter-house at Punta-Arenas."

"How do *you* manage to keep honest?" I asked, smiling.

"I don't take any chances," exclaimed the captain seriously.
"When I'm in their damned port I don't go ashore."

I did not again see Schnitzel until, with haggard eyes and
suspiciously wet hair, he joined the captain, doctor, purser,
and myself at breakfast. In the phrases of the Tenderloin, he
told us cheerfully that he had been grandly intoxicated, and to
recover drank mixtures of raw egg, vinegar, and red pepper,
the sight of which took away every appetite save his own.
When to this he had added a bottle of beer, he declared himself a new man. The new man followed me to the deck, and
with the truculent bearing of one who expects to be repelled,
he asked if, the day before, he had not made a fool of himself.

I suggested he had been somewhat confidential.

At once he recovered his pose and patronised me.

"Don't you believe it," he said. "That's all part of my
game. 'Confidence for confidence' is the way I work it.
That's how I learn things. I tell a man something on the inside, and he says: 'Here's a nice young fellow. Nothing
stand-offish about him', and he tells me something he
shouldn't. Like as not what I told him wasn't true. See?"

I assured him he interested me greatly.

"You find, then, in your line of business," I asked, "that

apparent frankness is advisable? As a rule," I explained, "secrecy is what a—a person in your line—a——"

To save his feelings I hesitated at the word.

"A spy," he said. His face beamed with fatuous complacency.

"But if I had not known you were a spy," I asked, "would not that have been better for you?"

"In dealing with a party like you, Mr Crosby," Schnitzel began sententiously, "I use a different method. You're on a secret mission yourself, and you get your information about the nitrate row one way, and I get it another. I deal with you just like we were drummers in the same line of goods. We are rivals in business, but outside of business hours perfect gentlemen."

In the face of the disbelief that had met my denials of any secret mission, I felt to have Schnitzel also disbelieve me would be too great a humiliation. So I remained silent.

"You make your report to the State Department," he explained, "and I make mine to—my people. Who they are doesn't matter. You'd like to know, and I don't want to hurt your feelings, but—that's *my* secret."

My only feelings were a desire to kick Schnitzel heavily, but for Schnitzel to suspect that was impossible. Rather, he pictured me as shaken by his disclosures.

As he hung over the rail the glare of the sun on the tumbling water lit up his foolish, mongrel features, exposed their cunning, their utter lack of any character, and showed behind the shifty eyes the vacant, half-crooked mind.

Schnitzel was smiling to himself with a smile of complete self-satisfaction. In the light of his later conduct, I grew to understand that smile. He had anticipated a rebuff, and he had been received, as he read it, with consideration. The irony of my politeness he had entirely missed. Instead, he read in what I said the admiration of the amateur for the professional.

He saw what he believed to be a high agent of the Government treating him as a worthy antagonist. In no other way
can I explain his later heaping upon me his confidences. It was
the vanity of a child trying to show off.

In ten days, in the limited area of a two-thousand-ton
steamer, one could not help but learn something of the history
of so communicative a fellow-passenger as Schnitzel. His
parents were German and still lived in Germany. But he himself had been brought up on the East Side. An uncle who kept
a delicatessen shop in Avenue A had sent him to the public
schools and then to a "business college", where he had
developed remarkable expertness as a stenographer. He re-
ferred to his skill in this difficult exercise with pitying contempt. Nevertheless, from a room noisy with typewriters this
skill had lifted him into the private office of the president of
the Nitrate Trust. There, as Schnitzel expressed it, "I saw
'mine', and I took it." To trace back the criminal instinct
that led Schnitzel to steal and sell the private letters of his
employer was not difficult. In all of his few early years I
found it lying latent. Of every story he told of himself, and
he talked only of himself, there was not one that was not to his
discredit. He himself never saw this, nor that all he told me
showed he was without the moral sense, and with an instinc-
tive enjoyment of what was deceitful, mean, and underhand.
That, as I read it, was his character.

In appearance he was smooth-shaven, with long locks that
hung behind wide, protruding ears. He had the unhealthy
skin of bad blood, and his eyes, as though the daylight hurt
them, constantly opened and shut. He was like hundreds of
young men that you see loitering on upper Broadway and
making predatory raids along the Rialto. Had you passed
him in that neighbourhood you would have set him down as
a wire-tapper, a racing tout, a would-be actor.

As I worked it out, Schnitzel was a spy because it gave him

an importance he had not been able to obtain by any other effort. As a child and as a clerk, it was easy to see that among his associates Schnitzel must always have been the butt. Until suddenly, by one dirty action, he had placed himself outside their class. As he expressed it: "Whenever I walk through the office now, where all the stenographers sit, you ought to see those slobs look after me. When they go to the president's door, they got to knock, like I used to, but now, when the old man sees me coming to make my report after one of these trips he calls out, 'Come right in, Mr Schnitzel.' And like as not I go in with my hat on and offer him a cigar. An' they see me do it, too!"

To me, that speech seemed to give Schnitzel's view of the values of his life. His vanity demanded he be pointed at, if even with contempt. But the contempt never reached him— he only knew that at last people took note of him. They no longer laughed at him, they were afraid of him. In his heart he believed that they regarded him as one who walked in the dark places of world politics, who possessed an evil knowledge of great men as evil as himself, as one who by blackmail held public ministers at his mercy.

This view of himself was the one that he tried to give me. I probably was the first decent man who ever had treated him civilly, and to impress me with his knowledge he spread that knowledge before me. It was *sale*, shocking, degrading.

At first I took comfort in the thought that Schnitzel was a liar. Later, I began to wonder if all of it were a lie, and finally, in a way I could not doubt, it was proved to me that the worst he charged was true.

The night I first began to believe him was the night we touched at Cristobal, the last port in Valencia. In the most light-hearted manner he had been accusing all concerned in the nitrate fight with every crime known in Wall Street and in the dark reaches of the Congo River.

"But I know him, Mr Schnitzel," I said sternly. "He is incapable of it. I went to college with him."

"I don't care whether he's a rah-rah boy or not," said Schnitzel, "I know that's what he did when he was up the Orinoco after orchids, and if the tribe had ever caught him they'd have crucified him. And I know this, too: he made forty thousand dollars out of the Nitrate Company on a ten-thousand-dollar job. And I know it, because he beefed to me about it himself, because it wasn't big enough."

We were passing the limestone island at the entrance to the harbour, where, in the prison fortress, with its muzzle-loading guns pointing drunkenly at the sky, are buried the political prisoners of Valencia.

"Now, there," said Schnitzel, pointing, "that shows you what the Nitrate Trust can do. Judge Rojas is in there. He gave the first decision in favour of the Walker-Keefe people, and for making that decision William T. Scott, the Nitrate manager, made Alvarez put Rojas in there. He's seventy years old, and he's been there five years. The cell they keep him in is below the sea-level, and the salt-water leaks through the wall. I've seen it. That's what William T. Scott did, an' up in New York people think 'Billy' Scott is a fine man. I seen him at the Horse Show sitting in a box, bowing to everybody, with his wife sitting beside him, all hung out with pearls. An' that was only a month after I'd seen Rojas in that sewer where Scott put him."

"Schnitzel," I laughed, "you certainly are a magnificent liar."

Schnitzel showed no resentment.

"Go ashore and look for yourself," he muttered. "Don't believe me. Ask Rojas. Ask the first man you meet." He shivered, and shrugged his shoulders. "I tell you, the walls are damp, like sweat."

The Government had telegraphed the commandant to

come on board and, as he expressed it, "offer me the hospitality of the port", which meant that I had to take him to the smoking-room and give him champagne. What the Government really wanted was to find out whether I was still on board, and if it were finally rid of me.

I asked the official concerning Judge Rojas.

"Oh, yes," he said readily. "He is still *incomunicado*."

Without believing it would lead to anything, I suggested: "It was foolish of him to give offence to Mr Scott?"

The commandant nodded vivaciously.

"Mr Scott is very powerful man," he assented. "We all very much love Mr Scott. The president, he love Mr Scott, too, but the judges were not sympathetic to Mr Scott, so Mr Scott asked our president to give them a warning, and Señor Rojas—he is the warning."

"When will he get out?" I asked.

The commandant held up the glass in the sunlight from the open air-port, and gazed admiringly at the bubbles.

"Who can tell?" he said. "Any day when Mr Scott wishes. Maybe, never. Señor Rojas is an old man. Old, and he has much rheumatics. Maybe, he will never come out to see our beloved country any more."

As we left the harbour we passed so close that one could throw a stone against the wall of the fortress. The sun was just sinking and the air became suddenly chilled. Around the little island of limestone the waves swept through the seaweed and black manigua up to the rusty bars of the cells. I saw the barefooted soldiers smoking upon the sloping ramparts, the common criminals in a long stumbling line bearing kegs of water, three storm-beaten palms rising like gallows, and the green and yellow flag of Valencia crawling down the staff. Somewhere entombed in that blotched and mildewed masonry an old man of seventy years was shivering and hugging himself from the damp and cold. A man who spoke five languages, a just, brave gentleman. To me it was no new story. I knew of the horrors of Cristobal prison; of political rivals chained to criminals loathsome with disease, of men who had raised the flag of revolution driven to suicide. But never had I supposed that my own people could reach from the city of New York and cast a fellow-man into that cellar of fever and madness.

As I watched the yellow wall sink into the sea, I became conscious that Schnitzel was near me, as before, leaning on the rail, with his chin sunk on his arms. His face was turned towards the fortress, and for the first time since I had known him it was set and serious. And when, a moment later, he passed me without recognition, I saw that his eyes were filled with fear.

When we touched at Curaçao I sent a cable to my sister, announcing the date of my arrival, and then continued on to the Hotel Venezuela. Almost immediately Schnitzel joined me. With easy carelessness he said: "I was in the cable office just now, sending off a wire, and that operator told me he can't make head or tail of the third word in your cable."

"That is strange," I commented, "because it's a French word, and he is French. That's why I wrote it in French."

With the air of one who nails another in a falsehood, Schnitzel exclaimed:

"Then, how did you suppose your sister was going to read it? It's a cipher, that's what it is. Oh, no, *you're* not on a secret mission! Not at all!"

It was most undignified of me, but in five minutes I excused myself, and sent to the State Department the following words:

"Roses red, violets blue, send snow."

Later at the State Department the only person who did not eventually pardon my jest was the clerk who had sat up until three in the morning with my cable, trying to fit it to any known code.

Immediately after my return to the Hotel Venezuela Schnitzel excused himself, and half an hour later returned in triumph with the cable operator and ordered lunch for both. They imbibed much sweet champagne.

When we again were safe at sea, I said: "Schnitzel, how much did you pay that Frenchman to let you read my second cable?"

Schnitzel's reply was prompt and complacent.

"One hundred dollars gold. It was worth it. Do you want to know how I doped it out?"

I even challenged him to do so.

" 'Roses red'—war declared; 'violets blue'—outlook bad, or blue; 'send snow'—send squadron, because the white squadron is white like snow. See? It was too easy."

"Schnitzel," I cried, "you are wonderful!"

Schnitzel yawned in my face.

"Oh, you don't have to hit the soles of my feet with a night-stick to keep me awake," he said.

After I had been a week at sea, I found that either I had to believe that in all things Schnitzel was a liar, or that the men of the Nitrate Trust were in all things evil. I was convinced that instead of the people of Valencia robbing them, they were robbing both the people of Valencia and the people of the United States.

To go to war on their account was to degrade our Government. I explained to Schnitzel it was not becoming that the United States navy should be made the cat's-paw of a corrupt corporation. I asked his permission to repeat to the authorities at Washington certain of the statements he had made.

Schnitzel was greatly pleased.

"You're welcome to tell 'em anything I've said," he assented. "And," he added, "most of it's true, too."

I wrote down certain charges he had made, and added what I had always known of the nitrate fight. It was a terrible arraignment. In the evening I read my notes to Schnitzel, who, in a corner of the smoking-room, sat frowning importantly, checking off each statement, and where I made an error of a date or a name, severely correcting me.

Several times I asked him, "Are you sure this won't get you into trouble with your 'people'? You seem to accuse everybody on each side."

Schnitzel's eyes instantly closed with suspicion.

"Don't you worry about me and my people," he returned sulkily. "That's *my* secret, and you won't find it out, neither. I may be as crooked as the rest of them, but I'm not giving away my employer."

I suppose I looked puzzled.

"I mean not a second time," he added hastily. "I know what you're thinking of, and I got five thousand dollars for it. But now I mean to stick by the men that pay my wages."

"But you've told me enough about each of the three to put any one of them in jail."

"Of course I have," cried Schnitzel triumphantly. "If I'd let down on any one crowd you'd know I was working for that crowd, so I've touched 'em all up. Only what I told you about my crowd—isn't true."

The report we finally drew up was so sensational that I was of a mind to throw it overboard. It accused members of the Cabinet, of our Senate, diplomats, business men of national interest, judges of the Valencia courts, private secretaries, clerks, hired bullies, and filibusters. Men the trust could not bribe it had blackmailed. Those it could not corrupt, and they were pitifully few, it crushed with some disgraceful charge.

Looking over my notes, I said:

"You seem to have made every charge except murder."

"How'd I come to leave that out?" Schnitzel answered flippantly. "What about Coleman, the foreman at Bahia, and that German contractor, Ebhardt, and old Smedburg? They talked too much, and they died of yellow-fever, maybe, and maybe what happened to them was they ate knock-out drops in their soup."

I disbelieved him, but there came a sudden nasty doubt.

"Curtis, who managed the company's plant at Barcelona, died of yellow-fever," I said, "and was buried the same day."

For some time Schnitzel glowered uncertainly at the bulk-head.

"Did you know him?" he asked.

"When I was in the legation I knew him well," I said.

"So did I," said Schnitzel. "He wasn't murdered. He murdered himself. He was wrong ten thousand dollars in his accounts. He got worrying about it and we found him outside the clearing with a hole in his head. He left a note saying he couldn't bear the disgrace. As if the company would hold a little grafting against as good a man as Curtis!"

Schnitzel coughed, and pretended it was his cigarette.

"You see you don't put in nothing against him," he added savagely.

It was the first time I had seen Schnitzel show emotion, and I was moved to preach.

"Why don't you quit?" I said. "You had an A 1 job as a stenographer. Why won't you go back to it?"

"Maybe, some day. But it's great being your own boss. If I was a stenographer, I wouldn't be helping you send in a report to the State Department, would I? No, this job is all right. They send you after something big, and you have the devil of a time getting it, but when you get it, you feel like you had picked a hundred-to-one shot."

The talk or the drink had elated him. His fish-like eyes bulged and shone. He cast a quick look about him. Except for ourselves, the smoking-room was empty. From below came the steady throb of the engines, and from outside the whisper of the waves and of the wind through the cordage. A barefooted sailor pattered by to the bridge. Schnitzel bent toward me, and with his hand pointed to his throat.

"I've got papers on me that's worth a million to a certain party," he whispered. "You understand, my notes in cipher."

He scowled with intense mystery.

"I keep 'em in an oiled-silk bag, tied around my neck with a string. And here," he added hastily, patting his hip, as though to forestall any attack I might make upon his person, "I carry my automatic. It shoots nine bullets in five seconds. They got to be quick to catch me."

"Well, if you have either of those things on you," I said testily, "I don't want to know it. How often have I told you not to talk and drink at the same time?"

"Ah, go on," laughed Schnitzel. "That's an old gag, warning a fellow not to talk so as to *make* him talk. I do that myself."

That Schnitzel had important papers tied to his neck I no more believe than that he wore a shirt of chain armour; but to please him I pretended to be greatly concerned.

"Now that we're getting into New York," I said, "you must be very careful. A man who carried such important documents on his person might be murdered for them. I think you ought to disguise yourself."

A picture of my bag being carried ashore by Schnitzel in the uniform of a ship's steward rather pleased me.

"Go on, you're kidding!" said Schnitzel. He was drawn between believing I was deeply impressed and with fear that I was mocking him.

"On the contrary," I protested, "I don't feel quite safe myself. Seeing me with you they may think I have papers around *my* neck."

"They wouldn't look at you," Schnitzel reassured me. "They know you're just an amateur. But, as you say, with me, it's different. I *got* to be careful. Now, you mightn't believe it, but I never go near my uncle nor none of my friends that live where I used to hang out. If I did, the other spies would get on my track. I suppose," he went on grandly, "I never go out in New York but that at least two spies are trailing me. But I know how to throw them off. I live 'way down town in a little hotel you never heard of. You never catch me dining at Sherry's nor the Waldorf. And you never met me out socially, did you, now?"

I confessed I had not.

"And then, I always live under an assumed name."

"Like 'Jones'?" I suggested.

"Well, sometimes 'Jones'," he admitted.

"To me," I said, " 'Jones' lacks imagination. It's the sort of name you give when you're arrested for exceeding the speed limit. Why don't you call yourself Machiavelli?"

"Go on, I'm no dago," said Schnitzel, "and don't you go off thinking 'Jones' is the only disguise I use. But I'm not tellin' what it is, am I? Oh, no."

"Schnitzel," I asked, "have you ever been told that you would make a great detective?"

"Cut it out," said Schnitzel. "You've been reading those fairy stories. There's no fly cops nor Pinks could do the work I do. They're pikers compared to me. They chase petty-larceny cases and kick in doors. I wouldn't stoop to what they do. It's being mixed up the way I am with the problems of two governments that catches me." He added magnanimously, "You see something of that yourself."

We left the ship at Brooklyn, and with regret I prepared to bid Schnitzel farewell. Seldom had I met a little beast so offensive, but his vanity, his lies, his moral blindness, made one pity him. And in ten days in the smoking-room together we had had many friendly drinks and many friendly laughs. He was going to a hotel on lower Broadway, and as my cab, on my way uptown, passed the door, I offered him a lift. He appeared to consider the advisability of this, and then, with much by-play of glancing over his shoulder, dived into the front seat and drew down the blinds. "This hotel I am going to is an old-fashioned trap," he explained, "but the clerk is wise to me, understand, and I don't have to sign the register."

As we drew nearer to the hotel, he said: "It's a pity we can't dine out somewhere and go to the theatre, but—you know?"

With almost too much heartiness I hastily agreed it would be imprudent.

"I understand perfectly," I assented. "You are a marked man. Until you get those papers safe in the hands of your 'people', you must be very cautious."

"That's right," he said. Then he smiled craftily.

"I wonder if you're on yet to which my people are."

I assured him that I had no idea, but that from the avidity with which he had abused them I guessed he was working for the Walker-Keefe crowd.

He both smiled and scowled.

"Don't you wish you knew?" he said. "I've told you a lot of inside stories, Mr Crosby, but I'll never tell on my pals again. Not me! That's *my* secret."

At the door of the hotel he bade me a hasty good-bye, and for a few minutes I believed that Schnitzel had passed out of my life forever. Then, in taking account of my belongings, I missed my field-glasses. I remembered that, in order to open a trunk for the customs inspectors, I had handed them to Schnitzel, and that he had hung them over his shoulder. In our haste at parting we both had forgotten them.

I was only a few blocks from the hotel, and I told the man to return.

I inquired for Mr Schnitzel, and the clerk, who apparently knew him by that name, said he was in his room, number eighty-two.

"But he has a caller with him now," he added. "A gentleman was waiting for him, and's just gone up."

I wrote on my card why I had called, and soon after it had been borne skyward the clerk said: "I guess he'll be able to see you now. That's the party that was calling on him, there."

He nodded toward a man who crossed the rotunda quickly. His face was twisted from us, as though, as he almost ran toward the street, he were reading the advertisements on the wall. He reached the door, and was lost in the great tide of Broadway.

I crossed to the elevator, and as I stood waiting, it descended with a crash, and the boy who had taken my card flung himself, shrieking, into the rotunda.

"That man—stop him!" he cried. "The man in eighty-two—he's murdered."

The clerk vaulted the desk and sprang into the street, and I dragged the boy back to the wire rope and we shot to the third story. The boy shrank back. A chambermaid, crouching against the wall, her face colourless, lowered one hand, and pointed at an open door.

"In there," she whispered.

In a mean, common room, stretched where he had been struck back upon the bed, I found the boy who had elected to meddle in the 'problems of two governments'.

In tiny jets, from three wide knife-wounds, his blood flowed slowly. His staring eyes were lifted up in fear and in entreaty. I knew that he was dying, and as I felt my impotence to help him, I as keenly felt a great rage and a hatred toward those who had struck him.

I leaned over him until my eyes were only a few inches from his face.

"Schnitzel?" I cried. "Who did this? You can trust me. Who did this? Quick!"

I saw that he recognised me, and that there was something

which, with terrible effort, he was trying to make me under-stand.

In the hall was the rush of many people, running, exclaim-ing, the noise of bells ringing; from another floor the voice of a woman shrieked hysterically.

At the sounds the eyes of the boy grew eloquent with en-treaty, and with a movement that called from each wound a fresh outburst, like a man strangling, he lifted his fingers to his throat.

Voices were calling for water, to wait for the doctor, to wait for the police. But I thought I understood.

Still doubting him, still unbelieving, ashamed of my own credulity, I tore at his collar, and my fingers closed upon a package of oiled silk.

I stooped, and with my teeth ripped it open, and holding before him the slips of paper it contained, tore them into tiny shreds.

The eyes smiled at me with cunning, with triumph, with deep content.

It was so like the Schnitzel I had known that I believed still he might have strength enough to help me.

"Who did this?" I begged. "I'll hang him for it! Do you hear me?" I cried.

Seeing him lying there, with the life cut out of him, swept me with a blind anger, with a need to punish.

"I'll see they hang for it. Tell me!" I commanded. "Who did this?"

The eyes, now filled with weariness, looked up and the lips moved freely.

"My own people," he whispered.

In my indignation I could have shaken the truth from him. I bent closer.

"Then, by God," I whispered back, "you'll tell me who they are!"

The eyes flashed sullenly.

"That's my secret," said Schnitzel.

The eyes set and the lips closed.

A man at my side leaned over him, and drew the sheet across his face.

RICHARD HARDING DAVIS

38. HOW IT STRIKES A CONTEMPORARY

I ONLY knew one poet in my life:
And this, or something like it, was his way.

You saw go up and down Valladolid,
A man of mark, to know next time you saw.
His very serviceable suit of black
Was courtly once and conscientious still,
And many might have worn it, though none did:
The cloak, that somewhat shone and showed the
    threads,
Had purpose, and the ruff, significance.
He walked and tapped the pavement with his cane,
Scenting the world, looking it full in face,
An old dog, bald and blindish, at his heels.
They turned up, now, the alley by the church,
That leads nowhither; now, they breathed themselves
On the main promenade just at the wrong time:
You'd come upon his scrutinising hat,
Making a peaked shade blacker than itself
Against the single window spared some house
Intact yet with its mouldered Moorish work,—
Or else surprise the ferrel of his stick

Trying the mortar's temper 'tween the chinks
Of some new shop a-building, French and fine.
He stood and watched the cobbler at his trade,
The man who slices lemons into drink,
The coffee-roaster's brazier, and the boys
That volunteer to help him turn its winch.
He glanced o'er books on stalls with half an eye,
And fly-leaf ballads on the vendor's string,
And broad-edge bold-print posters by the wall.
He took such cognisance of men and things,
If any beat a horse, you felt he saw;
If any cursed a woman, he took note;
Yet stared at nobody,—you stared at him,
And found, less to your pleasure than surprise,
He seemed to know you and expect as much.
So, next time that a neighbour's tongue was loosed,
It marked the shameful and notorious fact,
We had among us, not so much a spy,
As a recording chief-inquisitor,
The town's true master if the town but knew!
We merely kept a governor for form,
While this man walked about and took account
Of all thought, said and acted, then went home,
And wrote it fully to our Lord the King
Who has an itch to know things, he knows why,
And reads them in his bedroom of a night.
Oh, you might smile! there wanted not a touch,
A tang of . . . well, it was not wholly ease
As back into your mind the man's look came
Stricken in years a little,—such a brow
His eyes had to live under!—clear as flint
On either side the formidable nose
Curved, cut and coloured like an eagle's claw.
Had he to do with A.'s surprising fate?

When altogether old B. disappeared
And young C. got his mistress,—was't our friend,
His letter to the King, that did it all?
What paid the bloodless man for so much pains?
Our Lord the King has favourites manifold,
And shifts his ministry some once a month;
Our city gets new governors at whiles,—
But never word or sign, that I could hear,
Notified to this man about the streets
The King's approval of those letters conned
The last thing duly at the dead of night.
Did the man love his office? Frowned our Lord,
Exhorting when none heard—"Beseech me not!
"Too far above my people,—beneath me!
"I set the watch,—how should the people know?
"Forget them, keep me all the more in mind!"
Was some such understanding 'twixt the two?

    I found no truth in one report at least—
That if you tracked him to his home, down lanes
Beyond the Jewry, and as clean to pace,
You found he ate his supper in a room
Blazing with lights, four Titians on the wall,
And twenty naked girls to change his plate!
Poor man, he lived another kind of life
In that new stuccoed third house by the bridge,
Fresh-painted, rather smart than otherwise!
The whole street might o'erlook him as he sat,
Leg crossing leg, one foot on the dog's back,
Playing a decent cribbage with his maid
(Jacynth, you're sure her name was) o'er the cheese
And fruit, three red halves of starved winter-pears,
Or treat of radishes in April. Nine,
Ten, struck the church clock, straight to bed went he.

My father, like the man of sense he was,
Would point him out to me a dozen times;
" 'St-'St" he'd whisper, "the Corregidor!"
I had been used to think that personage
Was one with lacquered breeches, lustrous belt,
And feathers like a forest in his hat,
Who blew a trumpet and proclaimed the news,
Announced the bull-fights, gave each church its turn,
And memorised the miracle in vogue!
He had a great observance from us boys;
We were in error; that was not the man.

I'd like now, yet had haply been afraid,
To have just looked, when this man came to die,
And seen who lined the clean gay garret-sides
And stood about the neat low truckle-bed,
With the heavenly manner of relieving guard.
Here had been, mark, the general-in-chief,
Thro' a whole campaign of the world's life and death,
Doing the King's work all the dim day long,
In his old coat and up to knees in mud,
Smoked like a herring, dining on a crust,—
And, now the day was won, relieved at once!
No further show or need for that old coat,
You are sure, for one thing! Bless us, all the while
How sprucely we are dressed out, you and I!
A second, and the angels alter that.
Well, I could never write a verse,—could you?
Let's to the Prado and make the most of time.

ROBERT BROWNING

Some Simple Disguises

For a quick change it is wonderful what difference is made by merely altering your hat and necktie.

SIR ROBERT BADEN-POWELL

The above sketch shows the writer [Sir Robert Baden-Powell] in a tight place. He was discovered in close proximity to a rifle range by a German sentry. He pretended to be intoxicated and so escaped. But it was a close shave.

39. COULD NOT BELIEVE HIS EYES

IT fell to my lot at one time to live as a plumber in south-east London, and I grew a small "goatee" beard, which was rather in vogue amongst men of that class at that time.

One day, in walking past the Naval and Military Club in Piccadilly in my workman's get-up, I passed an old friend, a major in the Horse Artillery, and almost without thinking I accosted him by his regimental nickname. He stared and wondered, and then supposed that I had been a man in his battery, and could not believe his eyes when I revealed my identity.

SIR ROBERT BADEN-POWELL

40. NONE OTHER THAN . . .

AT that moment Sir Henry entered, and, catching sight of my companion, quickly removed his hat, bowed low, and expressed great regret at his absence.

"What does this mean?" I cried, amazed at the Ambassador's sudden obeisance to my companion.

"It means, Drew," he answered, turning to me, "it means that the man you know as Baron Engelhardt is none other than His Majesty the Emperor."

"The Emperor!" I gasped, gazing in wonderment as 'the Baron', laughing heartily, removed his false beard and readjusted his moustaches to their upward trend.

WILLIAM LE QUEUX

41. THE WAITERS' UNION

"WE are now," Guest declared, "in this position. In Hamburg I discovered the meeting place of the No. 1 Branch of the Waiters' Union, and the place itself is now under our control. In that room at the Café Suisse will be woven the final threads of the great scheme. How are we to get there? How are we to penetrate its secrets?"

"We must see the room first," I remarked.

"And then there is the question of ourselves," Guest continued. "We are both nominally dead men. But none the less, our friends leave little to chance. You may not have noticed it, but I knew very well that we were followed home today from the café. Every moment of ours will be spied upon. Is the change in our appearance sufficient?"

I looked at myself in the little gilt mirror over the mantelpiece. Perhaps because I looked, thinking of myself as I had been in the days before these strange happenings had come into my life, I answered his question promptly.

"I cannot believe," I said, "that any one would know me for Hardross Courage. I am perfectly certain, too, that I should not recognise in you today the Leslie Guest who—died at Saxby."

"I believe that you are right," Guest admitted. "At any rate, it is one of those matters which we must leave to chance. Only keep your identity always before you. At the Café Suisse, we shall be watched every moment of the day. Remember that you are a German-American of humble birth. Remember that always."

I nodded.

"I am not an impulsive person," I answered. "I am used to think before I speak. I shall remember. But there is one thing I am afraid of, Guest. It must also have occurred to you. Now that the Café Suisse is in the hands of strangers, will not your friends change their meeting place?"

"I think not," Guest answered slowly. "I know a little already about that room. It has a hidden exit, by way of the cellar, into a court, every house of which is occupied by foreigners. A surprise on either side would be exceedingly difficult. I do not think that our friends will be anxious to give up the place, unless their suspicions are aroused concerning us. You see their time is very close at hand now. This, at any rate, is another of the risks which we must run."

"Very well," I answered. "You see the time?"

Guest nodded.

"I am going to explain to you exactly," he said, "what you have to do."

"Right," I answered.

"The parcel on the sofa there," he said, "contains a second-hand suit of dress clothes. You will put them on, over them your old black overcoat which we bought at Hamburg, and your bowler hat. At four o'clock precisely, you will call at the offices of the German Waiters' Union, at No. 13, Old Compton Street, and ask for Mr Hirsch. Your name is Paul Schmidt. You were born in Offenbach, but went to America at the age of four. You were back in Germany for two years at the age of nineteen, and you have served your time at Mayence. You have come to England with an uncle, who has taken a small restaurant in Soho, and who proposes to engage you as head-waiter. You will be enrolled as a member of the Waiters' Union, as a matter of course; but when that has been arranged, you write on a slip of paper these words, and pass them to Mr Hirsch—'I, too, have a rifle'!"

I was beginning to get interested.

"'I, too, have a rifle'," I repeated. "Yes! I can remember that; but I shall be talking like a poll-parrot, for I shan't have the least idea what it means."

"You need not know much," Guest answered. "Those words are your passport into the No. 1 Branch of the Waiters' Union, whose committee, by the bye, meet at the Café Suisse. If you are asked why you wish to join, you need only say because you are a German!"

"Right," I answered. "I'll get into the clothes."

Guest gave me a few more instructions while I was changing and by four o'clock punctually I opened the swing door of No. 13, Old Compton Street. The place consisted of a waiting-room, very bare and very dirty; a counter, behind

which two or three clerks were very busy writing in ponderous, well-worn ledgers, and an inner door. I made my way
towards one of the clerks, and inquired in my best German if
I could see Mr Hirsch.

The clerk—he was as weedy a looking youth as ever I had
seen—pointed with ink-stained finger to the benches which
lined the room.

"You wait your turn," he said, and waved me away.

I took my place behind at least a dozen boys and young
men, whose avocation was unmistakable. Most of them were
smoking either cigarettes or a pipe, and most of them were
untidy and unhealthy-looking. They took no notice of me,
but sat watching the door to the inner room, which opened
and shut with wonderful rapidity. Every time one of their
number came out, another took his place. It came to my
turn sooner than I could have believed possible.

I found myself in a small office, untidy, barely furnished,
and thick with tobacco smoke. Its only occupant was a stout
man, with flaxen hair and beard, and mild blue eyes. He was
sitting in his shirt sleeves, and smoking a very black cigar.

"Well?" he exclaimed, almost before I had crossed the
threshold.

"My name is Paul Schmidt," I said, "and I should like to
join the Waiters' Union."

"Born?"

"Offenbach!"

"Age?"

"Thirty!"

"Working?"

"Café Suisse!"

"Come from?"

"America!"

He tossed me a small handbook.

"Half-a-crown," he said, holding out his hand.

I gave it him. I was beginning to understand why I had not been kept very long waiting.

"Clear out!" he said. "No questions, please. The book tells you everything!"

I looked him in the face.

"I, too, have a rifle," I said boldly.

I found, then, that those blue eyes were not so mild as they seemed. His glance seemed to cut me through and through.

"You understand what you are saying?" he asked.

"Yes!" I answered. "I want to join the No. 1 Branch."

"Why?"

"Because I am a German," I answered.

"Who told you about it?"

"A waiter named Hans in the Manhattan Hotel, New York." I lied with commendable promptitude.

"Have you served?" he asked.

"At Mayence, eleven years ago," I answered.

"Where did you say that you were working?" he asked.

"Café Suisse!" I said.

It seemed to me that he had been on the point of entering my name in a small ledger, which he had produced from one of the drawers by his side, but my answer apparently electrified him. His eyes literally held mine. He stared at me steadily for several moments.

"How long have you been there?" he asked. "I do not recognise you."

"I commence today," I said. "My uncle has just taken the café. He will make me his head-waiter."

"Has your uncle been in the business before?" he asked.

"He kept a saloon in Brooklyn," I answered.

"Made money at it?"

"Yes!"

"Were you with him?"

"No! I was at the Manhattan Hotel."

"Your uncle will not make a fortune at the Café Suisse," he remarked.

"I do not think," I answered, "that he will lose one."

"Does he know what you propose?"

I shook my head.

"The fatherland means little to him," I answered. "He has lived in America too long."

"You are willing to buy your own rifle?" he asked.

"I would rather not," I answered.

"We sell them for a trifle," he continued. "You would not mind ten shillings."

"I would rather pay nothing," I answered, "but I will pay ten shillings if I must."

He nodded.

"I cannot accept you myself," he said. "We know too little about you. You must attend before the committee tonight."

"Where?" I asked.

"At the Café Suisse," he answered. "We shall send for you! Till then!"

"Till then," I echoed, backing out of the room.

That night I gravely perambulated the little café in my waiter's clothes, and endeavoured to learn from Karl my new duties. There were a good many people dining there, but towards ten o'clock the place was almost empty. Just as the hour was striking, Mr Kauffman, who had been dining with Mr Hirsch, rose from his place, and with a key in his hand made his way towards the closed door.

He was followed by Mr Hirsch, and seven other men, all of whom had been dining at the long central table, which easily accommodated a dozen or more visitors. There was nothing at all remarkable about the nine men who shambled their way through the room. They did not in the least resemble conspirators. Hirsch, who was already smoking a huge pipe, touched me on the shoulder as he passed.

"We shall send for you presently," he declared. "Your case is coming before the committee."

I began checking some counterfoils at the desk, but before I had been there five minutes, the door of the inner room was opened, and Mr Hirsch appeared upon the threshold. He caught my eye and beckoned to me solemnly. I crossed the room, ascended the steps, and found myself in what the waiters called the club-room. Mr Hirsch carefully closed the door behind me.

The first thing that surprised me was, that although I had seen nine men ascend the three stairs and enter the room, there was now, besides myself and Hirsch, only one other person present. That other person was sitting at the head of the table, and he was of distinctly a different class from Hirsch and his friends. He was a young man, fair and well-built, and as obviously a soldier as though he were wearing his uniform. His clothes were well-cut, his hands shapely and white. Some instinct told me what to do. I stood to the salute, and I saw a glance of satisfaction pass between the two men.

"Your name is Paul Schmidt?" the man at the table asked me.

"Yes, sir!" I answered.

"You served at Mayence?"

"Yes, sir!"

"Under?"

"Colonel Hausman, sir, thirteenth regiment."

"You have your papers?"

I passed over the little packet which Guest had given me. My questioner studied them carefully, glancing up every now and then at me. Then he folded them up and laid them upon the table.

"You speak German with an English accent," he remarked, looking at me keenly.

"I have lived nearly all my life in America," I reminded him.

"You are sure," he said, "that you understand the significance of your request to join the No. 1 Branch of the Waiters' Union?"

"Quite sure, sir," I told him.

"Stand over there for a few minutes," he directed, pointing to the furthest corner of the room.

I obeyed, and he talked with Hirsch for several moments in an undertone. Then he turned once more to me.

"We shall accept you, Paul Schmidt," he said gravely. "You will come before the committee with us now."

I saluted, but said nothing. Hirsch pushed away the table, and, stooping down, touched what seemed to be a spring in the floor. A slight crack was instantly disclosed, which gradually widened until it disclosed a ladder. We descended, and found ourselves in a dry cellar, lit with electric lights. Seven men were sitting round a small table, in the furthest corner of the place. Their conversation was suspended as we appeared, and my interlocutor, leaving Hirsch and myself in the background, at once plunged into a discussion with them. I, too, should have followed him, but Hirsch laid his hand upon my arm.

"Wait a little," he whispered. "They will call us up."

"Who is he?" I asked, pointing to the tall military figure bending stiffly down at the table.

"Call him Captain X," Hirsch answered softly. "He does not care to be known here!"

"But how did he get into the room upstairs?" I asked. "I never saw him in the restaurant."

Hirsch smiled placidly.

"It is well," he said, "my young friend, that you do not ask too many questions!"

The man whom I was to call Captain X turned now and beckoned to me. I approached and stood at attention.

"I have accepted this man Paul Schmidt, as a member of the No. 1 Branch of the Waiters' Union," he announced. "Paul Schmidt, listen attentively, and you will understand in outline what the responsibilities are that you have undertaken."

There was a short silence. The men at the table looked at me, and I looked at them. I was not in any way ill-at-ease, but I felt a terrible inclination to laugh. The whole affair seemed to me a little ludicrous. There was nothing in the appearance of these men or the surroundings in the least impressive. They had the air of being unintelligent middle-class tradesmen of peaceable disposition, who had just dined to their fullest capacity, and were enjoying a comfortable smoke together. They eyed me amicably, and several of them nodded in a friendly way. I was forced to say something, or I must have laughed outright.

"I should like to know," I said, "what is expected of me."

An exceedingly fat man beckoned me to stand before him.

"Paul Schmidt," he said, "listen to me! You are a German born?"

"Without doubt," I answered.

"The love of your fatherland is still in your heart?"

"Always!" I answered fervently.

"Also with all of us," he answered. "You have lived in America so long, that a few words of explanation may be necessary. So!"

Now this man's voice, unimpressive though his appearance was, seemed somehow to create a new atmosphere in the place. He spoke very slowly, and he spoke as a man speaks of the things which are sacred to him.

"It is within the last few years," he said, "that all true patriots have been forced to realise one great and very ugly truth. Our country is menaced by an unceasing and untiring enmity. Wherever we have turned, we have met with its influence; whatever schemes for legitimate expansion our Kaiser and his great counsellors may have framed, have been checked, if not thwarted by our sleepless and relentless foe. No longer can we, the great peace-loving nation of the world, conceal from ourselves the coming peril. England has declared herself our sworn enemy!"

A little murmur of assent came from the other men. I neither spoke nor moved.

"There is but one end possible," he continued slowly. "It is war! It must come soon! Its shadow is all the time darkening the land. So we, who have understood the signs, remind one another that the Power who strikes the first blow, is the one who assures for herself the final success!"

Again he was forced to pause, for his breath was coming quickly. He lifted his long glass, and solemnly drained its contents. All the time, over its rim, his eyes held mine.

"So!" he exclaimed, setting it down with a little grunt of satisfaction. "It must be, then, Germany who strikes, Germany who strikes in self-defence. My young friend, there are in this country today 290,000 young countrymen of yours and mine who have served their time, and who can shoot. Shall these remain idle at such a time? No! We then have been at work. Clerks, tradesmen, waiters and hairdressers, each have their society, each have their work assigned to them. The forts which guard this great city may be impregnable from without, but from within—well, that is another matter. Listen! The exact spot where we shall attack is arranged, and plans of every fort which guard the Thames are in our hands. The signal will be—the visit of the British fleet to Kiel! Three days before, you will have your company assigned to you, and every possible particular. Yours it will be, and those of your comrades, to take a glorious part in the coming struggle! I drink with you, Paul Schmidt, and you, my friends, to that day!"

E. PHILLIPS OPPENHEIM

Professional Perquisites

Your visitation shall receive such thanks
As fits a king's remembrance.

WILLIAM SHAKESPEARE

42. ROYAL GIFTS

THAT night a Court official called upon me and handed me the ribbon and cross of the Order of the Black Eagle, with an autograph letter, together with the two hundred francs I had lent, and a present from the Princess Edna—the beautiful scarf-pin with the British royal cipher set in diamonds, which is now in my cravat as I write. Times without number have I been asked how the pin came into my possession, but until now I have always preserved the strictest silence.

*

The other day, before I left the castle, Her Serene Highness presented me with a relic of her devoted and well-beloved husband—the signet-ring of his royal house, which he had worn until that day when sorrow and remorse had fallen upon him. The ring, an antique gold one, is now upon my finger, a souvenir of the man who, knowing that death must overtake him suddenly, singled me out as his friend—the man with the black spectacles.

WILLIAM LE QUEUX

43. A WELL-APPOINTED OFFICE

IT might interest the reader to take a look into the office I occupied as head of the Foreign Department of the German Secret Service.

Entering the room, large, well-furnished and covered with a deep, luxurious carpet, the visitor would be faced by my big mahogany writing-desk. The most precious piece of furniture in the room was a big old-fashioned cupboard containing my personal reference library. To the left of the desk was a trolley-table covered with telephones and microphones connected directly with Hitler's Chancellery and other places of importance, one telephone providing a direct line to my home in Berlin, as well as to my country house in Herzberg. Microphones were hidden everywhere, in the walls, under the desk, even in one of the lamps, so that every conversation and every sound was automatically recorded. The windows of the room were covered with a wire mesh. This was an electrically charged safety device which was switched on at night and formed part of a system of photo-electric cells which sounded an alarm if anyone approached the windows, doors, safe, or, in fact, tried to get too close to any part of my offices. Within thirty seconds a squadron of armed guards would have surrounded the entire area.

My desk was like a small fortress. Two automatic guns were built into it which could spray the whole room with bullets. These guns pointed at the visitor and followed his or her progress towards my desk. All I had to do in an emergency was to press a button and both guns would fire simultaneously. At the same time I could press another button and a siren would summon the guards to surround the building and block every exit.

WALTER SCHELLENBERG

44. BLANC DE BLANC BRUT 1943

"AND now have you decided what you would like to have for dinner? Please be expensive," Bond added as he sensed her hesitation, "or you'll let down that beautiful frock."

"I'd made two choices," she laughed, "and either would

have been delicious, but behaving like a millionaire occasionally is a wonderful treat and if you're sure . . . well, I'd like to start with caviar and then have a plain grilled *rognon de veau* with *pommes soufflées*. And then I'd like to have *fraises des bois* with a lot of cream. Is it very shameless to be so certain and so expensive?" She smiled at him inquiringly.

"It's a virtue, and anyway, it's only a good plain wholesome meal." He turned to the *maître d'hôtel*, "and bring plenty of toast.

"The trouble always is," he explained to Vesper, "not how to get enough caviar, but how to get enough toast with it.

"Now," he turned back to the menu, "I myself will accompany mademoiselle with the caviar, but then I would like a very small *tournedos*, underdone, with *sauce Béarnaise* and a *cœur d'artichaut*. While mademoiselle is enjoying the strawberries, I will have half an avocado pear with a little French dressing. Do you approve?"

The *maître d'hôtel* bowed.

"My compliments, mademoiselle and monsieur. Monsieur George," he turned to the *sommelier* and repeated the two dinners for his benefit.

"*Parfait*," said the *sommelier*, proffering the leather-bound wine list.

"If you agree," said Bond, "I would prefer to drink champagne with you tonight. It is a cheerful wine and it suits the occasion—I hope," he added.

"Yes, I would like champagne," she said.

With his finger on the page, Bond turned to the *sommelier*: "The Taittinger '45?"

"A fine wine, monsieur," said the *sommelier*. "But if monsieur will permit," he pointed with his pencil, "the Blanc de Blanc Brut 1943 of the same *marque* is without equal."

Bond smiled. "So be it," he said.

"That is not a well-known brand," Bond explained to his companion, "but it is probably the finest champagne in the world."

IAN FLEMING

45. A CERTIFICATE FROM GENERAL WASHINGTON

ON entering an apartment that was apparently fitted for his reception, he took a seat, and continued for a long time in a thoughtful attitude, as one who was in the habit of communing much with himself. During this silence, the aide-de-camp sat in respectful expectation of his orders. At length the general raised his eyes, and spoke in the low placid tones that seemed natural to him.

"Has the man whom I wished to see arrived, sir?"

"He waits the pleasure of your Excellency."

"I will receive him here, and alone, if you please."

The aide bowed and withdrew. In a few minutes the door again opened, and a figure glided into the apartment, and stood modestly at a distance from the general, without speaking. His entrance was unheard by the officer, who sat gazing in the fire, deeply absorbed in his own meditations. Several minutes passed, when he spoke to himself in an undertone:

"Tomorrow we must raise the curtain, and expose our plans. May heaven prosper them!"

A slight movement made by the stranger at the sound of his voice caught his ear, and he turned his head and saw that he was not alone. He pointed silently to the fire, towards which the figure advanced, although the multitude of his garments, which seemed more calculated for disguise than comfort, rendered its warmth unnecessary—a second mild and courteous gesture motioned to a vacant chair, but the stranger refused it with a modest acknowledgment—another pause followed, and continued for some time; at length the officer arose and opening a desk that was laid upon the table near which he sat, took from it a small and apparently heavy bag.

"Harvey Birch," he said, turning to the stranger, "the time has arrived when our connection must cease; henceforth and for ever we must be strangers."

The pedlar dropped the folds of the great coat that concealed his features, and gazed for a moment wildly at the face of the speaker, and then dropping his head upon his bosom, said meekly:

"If it is your Excellency's pleasure."

"It is necessary—since I have filled the station which I now hold, it has become my duty to know many men, who, like yourself, have been my instruments in procuring intelligence—you have I trusted more than all; I early saw in you a regard to truth and principle that, I am pleased to say, has never deceived me—you alone know my secret agents in the city, and on your fidelity depends, not only their fortunes, but their lives."

He paused, as if to reflect, in order that full justice might be done to the pedlar, and then continued:

"I believe you are one of the very few that I have employed, who have acted faithfully to our cause; and while you have passed as a spy of the enemy's, have never given intelligence that you were not permitted to divulge; to me, and to me only of all the world, you seem to have acted with a strong attachment to the liberties of America."

During this address, Harvey had gradually raised his head from his bosom, until it reached the highest point of elevation; a faint tinge gathered in his cheeks, and as the officer concluded, it was diffused over his whole countenance in a deep glow, and he stood proudly swelling with his emotions, but with eyes that humbly sought the feet of the speaker.

"It is now my duty to pay you for your services—hitherto you have postponed receiving your reward, and the debt has become a heavy one—I wish not to under-value your dangers; here are an hundred joes—you will remember the poverty of our country, and attribute to it the smallness of your pay."

The pedlar raised his eyes to the countenance of the speaker with amazement, and as the other held forth the money, he moved back as if from contagion.

"It is not much for your services and risks, I acknowledge," said the general, "but it is all that I have to offer; at the end of the campaign, it may be in my power to increase it."

"Never!" said Birch, speaking out. "Was it for money that I did all this?"

"If not for money, what then?"

"What has brought your Excellency into the field? For what do you daily and hourly expose your precious life to battle and the halter? What is there about me to mourn, when such men as your Excellency risk their all for our country? No—no—no—not a dollar of your gold will I touch; poor America has need of it all!"

The bag dropped from the hand of the officer, and fell at the feet of the pedlar, where it lay neglected during the remainder of their interview. The officer looked steadily at the face of his companion, and continued:

"There are many motives which might govern me, that to you are unknown. Our situations are different; I am known as the leader of armies—but you must descend into the grave with the reputation of a foe to your native land. Remember, that the veil which conceals your true character cannot be raised in years—perhaps never."

Birch again lowered his face, but there was no yielding of the soul betrayed in the movement.

"You will soon be old; the prime of your days is already past; what have you to subsist on?"

"These!" said the pedlar, stretching forth his hands, that were already embrowned with toil.

"But those may fail you; take enough to secure a support to your age. Remember your risks and cares. I have told you, that the characters of men, who are much esteemed in life, depend upon your secrecy; what pledge can I give them of your fidelity?"

"Tell them," said Birch, advancing and unconsciously resting one foot on the bag, "tell them that I would not take the gold."

The composed features of the officer relaxed into a fine smile of benevolence, and he grasped the hand of the pedlar firmly.

"Now, indeed, I know you; and although the same reasons which have hitherto compelled me to expose your valuable life will still exist, and prevent my openly asserting your character, in private I can always be your friend—fail not to apply to me when in want or suffering, and so long as God giveth to me, so long will I freely share with a man who feels so nobly, and acts so well. If sickness or want should ever assail you, and peace once more smiles upon our efforts, seek the gate of him whom you have often met as Harper, and he will not blush to acknowledge you in his true character."

"It is little that I need in this life," said Harvey, the glow still mantling over his features. "So long as God gives me health and honest industry, I can never want in this happy country—but to know that your Excellency is my friend, is a blessing that I prize more than all the gold of England's treasury."

The officer stood for a few moments in the attitude of

intense thought. He then drew to him the desk, and wrote a few lines on a piece of paper, and gave it to the pedlar as he addressed him:

"That Providence destines this country to some great and glorious fate I must believe, while I witness the patriotism that pervades the bosoms of her lowest citizens. It must be dreadful to a mind like yours to descend into the grave, branded as a foe to liberty; but you already know the lives that would be sacrificed should your real character be revealed. It is impossible to do you justice now, but I fearlessly entrust you with this certificate—should we never meet again, it may be serviceable to your children."

"Children!" exclaimed the pedlar. "Can I give to a family the infamy of my name?"

The officer gazed at the strong emotion he exhibited with painful amazement, and made a slight movement towards the gold; but it was arrested by the proud expression of his companion's face. Harvey saw the intention, and shook his head, as he continued more mildly, and with an air of deep respect:

"It is indeed a treasure that your Excellency gives me—it is safe too. There are those living who could say that my life was nothing to me, compared to your secrets. The paper that I told you was lost, I swallowed when taken last by the Virginians. It was the only time I ever deceived your Excellency, and it shall be the last—yes, this is, indeed, a treasure to me—perhaps," he continued with a melancholy smile, "it may be known after my death who was my friend, and if it should not, there are none to grieve for me."

"Remember," said the officer with strong emotion, "that in me you will always have a secret friend: but openly I cannot know you."

"I know it—I know it," said Birch; "I knew it when I took the service. 'Tis probably the last time that I shall ever see your Excellency. May God pour down his choicest blessings on your head!" He paused, and moved towards the door. The officer followed him with eyes that expressed powerful interest. Once more the pedlar turned, and seemed to gaze on the placid, but commanding features of the general, with regret and reverence, and then, bowing low, he withdrew.

FENIMORE COOPER

Spare-Time Activities

Tea in the great hall, over which Lady Jocelyn presided, proved the usual irresponsible function.

WILLIAM LE QUEUX

46. PRISON READING

THE books I read during my three weeks in the Kremlin included: Thucydides, Renan's *Souvenirs d'Enfance et de Jeunesse*, Ranke's *History of the Popes*, Schiller's *Wallenstein*, Rostand's *L'Aiglon*, Archenholtz's *History of the Seven Years War*, Beltzke's *History of the War in Russia in 1812*, Sudermann's *Rosen*, Macaulay's *Life and Letters*, Stevenson's *Travels with a Donkey*, Kipling's *Captains Courageous*, Wells' *The Island of Doctor Moreau*, Holland Rose's *Life of Napoleon*, Carlyle's *French Revolution* and Lenin and Zinovieff's *Against the Current*. I was a serious young man in those days.

R. H. BRUCE LOCKHART

47. PLANNING A NOVEL

THE Colonel arrived, bursting with apologies, twenty minutes late, and hurried his guest straight into the restaurant. "We must have a whisky-soda immediately," he said and called loudly for a bottle of "Johnnie".

During most of the meal he talked about the detective stories he had read, his reactions to them, his opinions of the characters and his preference for murderers who shot their victims. At last, with an almost empty bottle of whisky at his elbow and a strawberry ice in front of him, he leaned forward across the table.

"I think, Mr Latimer," he said again, "that I can help you."

For one wild moment Latimer wondered if he were going

to be offered a job in the Turkish secret service; but he said:
"That's very kind of you."

"It was my ambition," continued Colonel Haki, "to write
a good *roman policier* of my own. I have often thought that
Icould do so if I had the time. That is the trouble—the time.
I have found that out. But . . ." He paused impressively.

Latimer waited. He was always meeting people who felt
that they could write detective stories if they had the time.

"But," repeated the Colonel, "I have the plot prepared; I
would like to make you a present of it."

Latimer said that it was very good indeed of him.

The Colonel waved away his thanks. "Your books have
given me so much pleasure, Mr Latimer. I am glad to make
you a present of an idea for a new one. I have not the time
to use it myself, and, in any case," he added magnanimously,
"you would make better use of it than I should."

Latimer mumbled incoherently.

"The scene of the story," pursued his host, his grey eyes
fixed on Latimer's, "is an English country house belonging to
the rich Lord Robinson. There is a party for the English
week-end. In the middle of the party, Lord Robinson is
discovered in the library sitting at his desk—shot through the
temple. The wound is singed. A pool of blood has formed on
the desk and it has soaked into a paper. The paper is a new
will which the Lord was about to sign. The old will divided
his money equally between six persons, his relations, who are
at the party. The new will, which he has been prevented
from signing by the murderer's bullet, leaves all to one of
those relations. Therefore"—he pointed his ice-cream spoon
accusingly—"one of the five other relations is the guilty
one. That is logical, is it not?"

Latimer opened his mouth, then shut it again and nodded.

Colonel Haki grinned triumphantly. "That is the trick."

"The trick?"

"The Lord was murdered by none of the suspects, but by the butler, whose wife had been seduced by this Lord! What do you think of that, eh?"

"Very ingenious."

His host leaned back contentedly and smoothed out his tunic. "It is only a trick, but I am glad you like it. Of course, I have the whole plot worked out in detail. The *flic* is a High Commissioner of Scotland Yard. He seduces one of the suspects, a very pretty woman, and it is for her sake that he solves the mystery. It is quite artistic. But, as I say, I have the whole thing written out."

ERIC AMBLER

48. LOVE

I HAVE been taken prisoner by the Americans, and stript of everything except the picture of Honora, which I concealed in my mouth. Preserving that, I yet think myself fortunate.

Letter from MAJOR ANDRÉ to one of his friends

A Gaggle of Suspects

My experience is that the gentlemen who are the best behaved and the most sleek are those who are doing the mischief. We cannot be too sure of anybody.

> THE COMMANDER-IN-CHIEF, HOME FORCES (Ironside), addressing Local Defence Volunteers on 5 June 1940

49. QUEER PEOPLE

LONDON is full of pigeons—wood pigeons in the parks, blue rocks about the churches and public buildings—and a number of amiable people take pleasure in feeding them. In September 1914, when this phase was at its height, it was positively dangerous to be seen in conversation with a pigeon; it was not always safe to be seen in its vicinity. A foreigner walking in one of the parks was actually arrested and sentenced to imprisonment because a pigeon was seen to fly from the place where he was standing and it was supposed that he had liberated it.

The delusion about illicit wireless ran the pigeons very hard. The pronouncement of a thoughtless expert that an aerial might be hidden in a chimney, and that messages could be received through an open window even on an iron bed-stead, gave a great impetus to this form of delusion. The high scientific authority of the popular play, *The Man Who Stayed at Home*, where a complete installation was concealed behind a fireplace, spread the delusion far and wide. It was idle to assure the sufferers that a Marconi transmitter needed a four-horsepower engine to generate the wave, that skilled operators were listening day and night for the pulsations of unauthorised messages, that the intermittent tickings they heard from the flat above them were probably the efforts of an amateur typist: the sufferers knew better. At this period the disease attacked even naval and military officers and special constables. If a telegraphist was sent on a motor-cycle to examine and test the telegraph poles, another cyclist was certain to be sent by some authority in pursuit. On one occasion the authorities dispatched to the Eastern Counties a

car equipped with a Marconi apparatus and two skilled operators to intercept any illicit messages that might be passing
over the North Sea. They left London at noon; at three they
were under lock and key in Essex. After an exchange of telegrams they were set free, but at 7 p.m. they telegraphed from
the police cells in another part of the country, imploring help.
When again liberated they refused to move without the escort
of a Territorial officer in uniform, but on the following morning the police of another county had got hold of them and
telegraphed, "Three German spies arrested with car and
complete wireless installation, one in uniform of British
officer."

Next in order was the German governess, also perhaps the
product of *The Man Who Stayed at Home*. There were
several variants of this story, but a classic version was that the
governess was missing from the midday meal, and that when
the family came to open her trunks they discovered under a
false bottom a store of high-explosive bombs. Everyone who
told this story knew the woman's employer; some had even
seen the governess herself in happier days—"Such a nice
quiet person, so fond of the children; but now one comes to
think of it, there was a something in her face, impossible to
describe, but a something."

During the German advance through Belgium an ingenious
war correspondent gave a new turn to the hysteria. He alleged
that the enamelled iron advertisements for "Maggi Soup",
which were to be seen attached to every hoarding and telegraph post, were unscrewed by the German officers in order
to read the information about the local resources, which was
painted in German on the back. Screwdriver parties were
formed in the London suburbs, and in destroying this delusion they removed also many unsightly advertisements. The
hallucination about gun platforms was not dispatched so
easily. As soon as a correspondent had described the gun

emplacements laid down by Germans in the guise of tennis courts at Mauberge there was scarcely a paved back-garden nor a flat concrete roof in London that did not come under the suspicion of some spy-maniac. The denunciations were not confined to Germans. Given a British householder with a concrete tennis-court and pigeons about the house, and it was certain to be discovered that he had quite suddenly increased the scale of his expenditure, that heavy cases had been delivered at the house by night, that tapping had been over-heard, mysterious lights seen in the windows, and that on the night of the sinking of the *Lusitania* he had given a dinner-party to naturalised Germans. When artillery experts assured the patients that gun emplacements in the heart of London were in the wrong place, and that even on the high lands of Sydenham or of Hampstead any tram road would better serve the purpose, they wagged their heads. They were hot upon the scent, and for many weeks denunciations poured in at the rate of many hundreds a day. . . .

A new phase of the malady was provoked by the suggestion that advertisements in the Agony Column of newspapers were being used by spies to communicate information to Germany. It is uncertain who first called public attention to this danger, but since refugees did make use of the Agony Columns for communicating with their friends abroad, there was nothing inherently improbable in the idea. In order to allay public alarm it was necessary to check the insertion of apparently cryptic advertisements. Later in the war a gentleman who had acquired a considerable reputation as a code expert, and was himself the author of commercial codes, began to read into these advertisements messages from German submarines to their base, and *vice versa*. This he did with the aid of a Dutch–English dictionary on a principle of his own. As we had satisfied ourselves about the authors of the advertisements we treated his communications rather lightly. In most cases

the movements he foretold failed to take place, but unfortunately once, by an accident, there did happen to be an air-raid
on the night foretold by him. We then inserted an advertisement of our own. It was something like this:

> Will the lady with the fur boa who entered No. 14 'bus
> at Hyde Park Corner yesterday afternoon communicate
> with Box 29.

and upon this down came our expert hot-foot with the information that six submarines were under orders to attack
the defences at Dover that very night. When we explained
that we were the authors of the advertisement, all he said was
that, by some extraordinary coincidence, we had hit upon the
German code, and that by inserting the advertisement we
had betrayed a military secret. It required a committee to
dispose of this delusion.

The longest-lived of the delusions was that of the night-
signalling, for whenever the scare showed signs of dying
down a Zeppelin raid was sure to give it a fresh start. As far
as fixed lights were concerned, it was the best-founded of all
the delusions, because the Germans might well have in-
augurated a system of fixed lights to guide Zeppelins to their
objective, but the sufferers went a great deal farther than a
belief in fixed lights. Morse-signalling from a window in
Bayswater, which could be seen only from a window on the
opposite side of the street, was believed in some way to be
conveyed to the commanders of German submarines in the
North Sea, to whom one had to suppose news from Bayswater was of paramount importance. Sometimes the watcher
—generally a lady—would call in a friend, a noted Morse
expert, who in one case made out the letters "P.K." among a
number of others that he could not distinguish. This phase
of the malady was the most obstinate of all. It was useless to
point out that a more sure and private method of conveying

information across a street would be to go personally or send a note. It was not safe to ignore any of these complaints, and all were investigated. In a few cases there were certainly intermittent flashes, but they proved to be caused by the flapping of a blind, the waving of branches across a window, persons passing across a room, and, in two instances, the quick movements of a girl's hairbrush in front of the light. The beacons were passage lights left unshrouded. . . .

On one occasion a very staid couple came down to denounce a waiter in one of the large hotels, and brought documentary evidence with them. It was a menu with a rough sketch plan in pencil made upon the back. They believed it to be a plan of Kensington Gardens with the Palace buildings roughly delineated by an oblong figure. They had seen the waiter in the act of drawing the plan at an unoccupied table. I sent for him and found before me a spruce little Swiss with his hair cut *en brosse*, and a general air of extreme surprise. He gave me a frank account of all his movements, and then I produced the plan. He gazed at it a moment, and then burst out laughing. "So that is where my plan went! Yes, monsieur, I made it, and then I lost it. You see, I am new to the hotel, and, in order to satisfy the head waiter, I made for myself privately a plan of the tables, and marked a cross against those I had to look after."

SIR BASIL THOMSON

50. THE LAWRENCES

In the growing atmosphere of suspicion and hostility generated by the [1914] war, D. H. Lawrence came to be looked upon as a dangerous person, partly because he wrote and had a beard, and partly because his wife was German. One wintry afternoon, when he and Frieda were going home, with their knapsack, two officers stopped them and asked what they were carrying. "A few groceries," Lawrence replied. One of the officers insisted on examining the contents, and pulling out what he thought to be a camera discovered it was a pound of salt. Two Americans, a man and a woman, visited Lawrence, and a police sergeant was sent round by the military to examine their papers, and when they returned to London, the man was taken to Scotland Yard, stripped and put in a cell for the night. The country people began to spy on the Lawrences: Frieda could not hang a towel on a bush, or carry out the slops without her movements being watched. When Lawrence had the chimney tarred to keep out the damp, the countryside agreed that it was a signal to the Germans. He and Frieda were supposed to supply German submarines with food, and with petrol stored in some recess of the cliffs. Cecil Gray came down to Cornwall, the Lawrences visited him, and one evening, while Lawrence was singing German songs to himself rather to Gray's discomfort, an officer banged on the door and strode in, followed by three local spies. The spies had reported a light seen through an uncurtained window, and though it turned out to be a candle held by the housekeeper on her way to her room, Cecil Gray was fined £20.

This niggling persecution wore Lawrence's nerves very thin. One day, when he and Frieda were sitting on some rocks by the sea, Frieda, exhilarated by the air and sun, jumped up and ran along, her white scarf streaming in the wind, while Lawrence screamed—"Stop it, stop it, you fool, you fool! Can't you see they'll think you are signalling to the enemy!" . . .

One day in October [1917] when he and Frieda were both out, the cottage was searched, and some papers and a book removed. The next morning an officer, a police sergeant, and two local men called, and the police sergeant read out an order from W. Western, Major-General i/c Administration, Southern Command, Salisbury, that Lawrence and his wife were to leave Cornwall for an unprohibited area, where they must report to the police on arrival.

HUGH KINGSMILL

51. OPERATION GOETHE

SURPRISED in Sweden by the war—if the word "surprise" is appropriate—we had a somewhat distressing, perhaps even perilous, trip home, first by air to London and then on the overcrowded *S.S. Washington*. I carried many papers, lecture notes, and books with me, which were the object of tedious inspection at the remote and camouflaged London airport. The inspecting officers were particularly suspicious of a sketch representing the seating arrangement at a dinner that Goethe gave in his house on the Frauenplan in Weimar in honour of the sweetheart of his youth. It was suspected of being of strategic importance, and I had to deliver a condensed lecture on the novel in order to convince the officials of the complete innocence of the paper.

THOMAS MANN

52. WHAT THE SOLDIER SAID

THE Soldier [John Scofield] said to Mrs Grinder, that it would be right to have my House searched, as I might have plans of the Country which I intended to send to the Enemy; he called me a Military Painter; I suppose mistaking the words

Miniature Painter, which he might have heard me called. I think that this proves, his having come into the Garden with some bad Intention, or at least with a prejudiced Mind.

*

BLAKE REPLIES

Go thou to Skofield: ask him if he is Bath or if he is Canter-
    bury.
Tell him to be no more dubious: demand explicit words.
Tell him I will dash him into shivers where and at what time
I please; tell Hand and Skofield they are my ministers of evil
To those I hate, for I can hate also as well as they!

WILLIAM BLAKE

53. COLERIDGE AND WORDSWORTH, SUSPECTS

THE dark guesses of some zealous *Quidnunc* met with so con-
genial a soil in the grave alarm of a titled Dogberry of our
neighbourhood, that a spy was actually sent down from the
government *pour surveillance* of myself and friend. There
must have been not only abundance, but variety of these
"honourable men" at the disposal of Ministers: for this
proved a very honest fellow. After three weeks' truly Indian
perseverance in tracking us (for we were commonly together),
during all which time seldom were we out of doors, but he
contrived to be within hearing—and all the while utterly unsuspected; how indeed *could* such a suspicion enter our
fancies?—he not only rejected Sir Dogberry's request that
he would try a little longer, but declared to him his belief, that
both my friend and myself were as good subjects, for aught he

could discover to the contrary, as any in His Majesty's
dominions. He had repeatedly hid himself, he said, for hours
together behind a bank at the seaside (our favourite seat), and
overheard our conversation. At first he fancied, that we were
aware of our danger; for he often heard me talk of one *Spy
Nozy*, which he was inclined to interpret of himself, and of a
remarkable feature belonging to him; but he was speedily
convinced that it was the name of a man who had made a book
and lived long ago. Our talk ran most upon books, and we
were perpetually desiring each other to look at *this*, and to
listen to *that*; but he could not catch a word about politics.
Once he had joined me on the road (this occurred, as I was
returning home alone from my friend's house, which was
about three miles from my own cottage), and, passing himself
off as a traveller, he had entered into conversation with me,
and talked of purpose in a democrat way in order to draw
me out. The result, it appears, not only convinced him that I
was no friend of jacobinism; but (he added), I had "plainly
made it out to be such a silly as well as wicked thing, that he
felt ashamed though he had only *put it on*." I distinctly remembered the occurrence, and had mentioned it immediately
on my return, repeating what the traveller with his Bardolph
nose had said, with my own answer; and so little did I suspect
the true object of my "tempter ere accuser", that I expressed
with no small pleasure my hope and belief, that the conversation had been of some service to the poor misled malcon-
tent. This incident therefore prevented all doubt as to the
truth of the report, which through a friendly medium came
to me from the master of the village inn, who had been
ordered to entertain the Government gentleman in his best
manner, but above all to be silent concerning such a person
being in his house. At length he received Sir Dogberry's
commands to accompany his guest at the final interview; and,
after the absolving suffrage of the *gentleman honoured with the*

confidence of Ministers, answered, as follows, to the following queries: D. Well, landlord! and what do you know of the person in question? L. I see him often pass by with maister ——, my landlord (*that is, the owner of the house*), and sometimes with the new-comers at Holford; but I never said a word to him or he to me. D. But do you not know, that he has distributed papers and hand-bills of a seditious nature among the common people? L. No, your Honour! I never heard of such a thing. D. Have you not seen this Mr Coleridge, or heard of, his haranguing and talking to knots and clusters of the inhabitants?—What are you grinning at, Sir? L. Beg your Honour's pardon! but I was only thinking, how they'd have stared at him. If what I have heard be true, your Honour! they would not have understood a word he said. When our Vicar was here, Dr. L. the master of the great school and Canon of Windsor, there was a great dinner party at maister ——'s; and one of the farmers, that was there, told us that he and the Doctor talked real Hebrew Greek at each other for an hour together after dinner. D. Answer the question, Sir! does he ever harangue the people? L. I hope your Honour an't angry with me. I can say no more than I know. I never saw him talking with any one, but my landlord, and our curate, and the strange gentleman. D. Has he not been seen wandering on the hills towards the Channel, and along the shore, with books and papers in his hand, taking charts and maps of the country? L. Why, as to that, your Honour! I own, I have heard; I am sure, I would not wish to say ill of any body; but it is certain, that I have heard—— D. Speak out, man! don't be afraid, you are doing your duty to your King and Government. What have you heard? L. Why, folks do say, your Honour! as how that he is a *Poet*, and that he is going to put Quantock and all about here in print; and as they be so much together, I suppose that the strange gentleman has some *consarn* in the business.—So ended this formidable inquisition, the latter part of which alone requires explanation, and at the same time entitles the anecdote to a place in my literary life.

S. T. COLERIDGE

The Agent Reports

11th Aug. My Lord Duke—On the 8th instant I took the liberty to acquaint your grace with a very suspicious business concerning an emigrant family, who have contrived to get possession of a Mansion House at Alfoxton, late belonging to the Revd Mr St Albyn under Quantock Hills. I am since informed that the Master of the house has no wife with him, but only a woman who passes for his sister. The man has Camp Stools which he and his visitors take with them when they go about the country upon their nocturnal or diurnal excursions and have also a Portfolio in which they enter their observations which they have been heard to say were almost finished. They have been heard to say they should be rewarded for them, and were very attentive to the River near them. . . . These people may *possibly* be under-agents to some principal in Bristol.

54. THE GENDARME AND THE PAINTER

I am drawing on the beach, on the frontier. A gendarme from the Midi, who suspects me of being a spy, says to me, who come from Orleans: "Are you French?"

"Why, certainly."

"That's odd. Vous n'avez pas l'accent (lakesent) français."

PAUL GAUGUIN

55. A LAWYER FROM KENT

LISBON, July 30th, 1940. Yesterday Windsor was with his Ambassador for a lengthy consultation. Today there arrived at the Duke's the English Minister who calls himself Sir Walter Turner Monckstone, a lawyer from Kent. The Portuguese confidential agent assumes, as I do too, that a cover name is involved. It is possible that it concerns a member of the personal police of the reigning King by the name of Camerone.

WALTER SCHELLENBERG (in a report to Berlin)

56. THE AMOROUS DUCHESS

NOVEMBER 10th, 1894. The intelligence service informed us in June last of a mysterious correspondence carried on daily in coded telegrams between the Count of Turin, a nephew of King Umberto of Italy, and the Duchessa Grazioli, an Italian living at the Hotel Windsor in Paris.

Colonel Sandherr,[1] like a true gendarme, said to me:

"These telegrams don't smell good to me; to me there's a whiff of espionage about them."

I answered:

"This time, my dear colonel, your flair is deceiving you. To me these coded telegrams seem to give off a delicious perfume, for I know the lady who sends or receives them, the beautiful Duchessa Grazioli, Donna Nicoletta. She is a superb creature, tall, supple, and as voluptuous as a Bacchante. All her days and all her nights are not long enough for the

[1] Chief of the French Intelligence Service.

caprices of her private life, and I assure you that she has something better to do with her time than to engage in espionage. ''

But my romantic explanation failed to convince Sandherr, a sceptic by profession.

Not long afterwards—it was on a Monday—he burst into my office, with a gleam of exhilaration in his eyes.

"Look!" he said, handing me a small, flat book bound in blue cloth. "Look! There's your duchess's cipher! I've brought it so that your decoders can have a look at her correspondence with the Count of Turin."

"How did you get hold of it?"

"Oh, that was easy! The Duchessa Grazioli lives at the Hotel Windsor. I had her watched by one of my agents. Well, yesterday, Sunday, she went to the races. My man took advantage of the opportunity to slip into her room and search her trunks, her wardrobes, her bed, her clothes . . .''

"And the hotel servants let him?"

"The hotel servants? Naturally I had given them something to keep their eyes shut."

"Naturally, that was the indispensable preliminary, I should have realised. . . . And the cipher?"

"In the end my agent found it in a very pretty toilet necessity, underneath a packet of fine handkerchiefs. Also it has a delicious scent. Smell it!"

"You're quite right, the scent is delicious. . . . You see how right I was the other day when I told you that your flair had deceived you!"

"Yes. . . . All that's left now is to see what is in the telegrams."

"Your curiosity shall soon be satisfied."

Two days later I took Sandherr the translation of his mysterious telegrams. Indeed they contained no suspicion of espionage. The decoded correspondence was perfectly clear and frank, for it expressed nothing but simple, elemental, natural feelings.

However, one four-figure sequence which recurred in most of the telegrams remained indecipherable. All that our decoders were able to suggest was that the apocalyptic number stood for something extraordinary, unforgettable, and sublime.

MAURICE PALÉOLOGUE

57. POSTSCRIPT TO DREYFUS

DREYFUS remained what he had always been, a strictly honourable soldier. He had never lent himself to political adventurers. After a short period in the Army, he resigned and went on to the reserve. During the 1914–18 war he was recalled to service and commanded an ammunition column with efficiency. He died in 1935, a quiet old gentleman During his later years he liked to play bridge. One evening his partner remarked that a certain X had been arrested for espionage, and then, realising the tactlessness of his remark, added that he did not suppose there was anything in it. Dreyfus, calmly dealing, rejoined: "Oh, I don't know; after all, there's no smoke without fire."

GUY CHAPMAN

Tricks of the Trade

Often most valuable clues can be picked up by
spies who get beneath windows and peer in at the
corners at critical times.

WILLIAM LE QUEUX

58. BENEATH THE OPEN WINDOWS

Scene: Tilsit and the river Niemen.

Napoléon and Alexander emerge from their seclusion, and each is beheld talking to the suite of his companion apparently in flattering compliment. An effusive parting, which signifies itself to be but temporary, is followed by their return to the river shores amid the cheers of the spectators. Napoléon and his marshals arrive at the door of his quarters and enter, and pass out of sight to other rooms than that of the foreground in which the observers are loitering. Dumb show ends. A murmured conversation grows audible, carried on by two persons in the crowd beneath the open windows. Their dress being the native one, and their tongue unfamiliar, they seem to the officers to be merely inhabitants gossiping; and their voices continue unheeded.

First English Spy:[1] Did you get much for me to send on?
Second English Spy: I have got hold of the substance of their parley. Surely no truce in European annals ever led to so odd an interview. They were like a belle and her beau, by God! But, queerly enough, one of Alexander's staff said to him as he reached the raft: "Sire, let me humbly ask you not to forget your father's fate!" Grim—eh?
First Spy: Anything about the little island which shall be nameless?
Second Spy: Much; and startling, too. "Why are we at war?" says Napoléon when they met.—"Ah—why!" said t'other.

[1] It has been conjectured of late that these adventurous spirits were Sir Robert Wilson and, possibly, Lord Hutchinson, present there at imminent risks of their lives.

—"Well," said Boney, "I am fighting you only as an ally of the English, and you are simply serving them, and not yourself, in fighting me."—"In that case," says Alexander, "we shall soon be friends, for I owe her as great a grudge as you."

First Spy: Dammy, go that length, did they!

Second Spy: Then they plunged into the old story about English selfishness, and greed, and duplicity. But the climax related to Spain, and it amounted to this: they agreed that the Bourbons of the Spanish throne should be made to abdicate, and Bonaparte's relations set up as sovereigns instead of them.

First Spy: Somebody must ride like hell to let our Cabinet know!

Second Spy: I have written it down in cipher, not to trust to memory, and to guard against accidents.—They also agreed that France should have the Pope's dominions, Malta, and Egypt; that Napoléon's brother Joseph should have Sicily as well as Naples, and that they would partition the Ottoman Empire between them.

First Spy: Cutting up Europe like a plum-pudding. *Par nobile fratrum!*

Second Spy: Then the worthy pair came to poor Prussia, whom Alexander, they say, was anxious about, as he is under engagements to her. It seems that Napoléon agrees to restore to the King as many of his states as will cover Alexander's promise, so that the Tsar may feel free to strike out in this new line with his new friend.

First Spy: Surely this is but surmise?

Second Spy: Not at all. One of the suite overheard, and I got round him. There was much more, which I did not learn. But they are going to soothe and flatter the unfortunate King and Queen by asking them to a banquet here.

First Spy: Such a spirited woman will never come!

Second Spy: We shall see. Whom necessity compels needs must; and she has gone through an Iliad of woes!

First Spy: It is this Spanish business that will stagger England, by God! And now to let her know it.

French Subaltern (*looking out above*): What are those townspeople talking about so earnestly, I wonder? The lingo of this place has an accent akin to English.

Second Subaltern: No doubt because the races are both Teutonic.

(The spies observe that they are noticed, and disappear in the crowd. The curtain drops.)

THOMAS HARDY

59. THE ORDINARY ROUTE

[Nisard was the Director of Political Affairs at the Quai D'Orsay; General Mercier, the Minister of War; Hanotaux, the Foreign Minister.]

OCTOBER 12th, 1894. When Nisard had come to the end of his confidences, he asked me if I knew how the intelligence service procured papers from the German Embassy. General Mercier had said that the letter had reached the General Staff by "the ordinary route". What was this "ordinary route"? Hanotaux attached great importance to being informed on this point.

I explained to him how the "ordinary route" worked.

"The intelligence service," I said, "has succeeded in suborning a servant at the German Embassy. She is a woman of about forty. Her name is Marie Bastian. She is vulgar, stupid, and completely illiterate, but she has been clever enough to gain the confidence of her employers. She is the charwoman; she washes down the stairs, cleans the windows, lights the fires, and sweeps out the offices, and she has the run of the house all day long. It is thus very easy for her to pick up papers which Embassy secretaries or military attachés tear up and put in the waste-paper basket. She periodically hands them over to another counter-espionage agent, Brücker, or sometimes to an officer of the intelligence service. The hand-over generally takes place in the evening, in a chapel of St Clotilda."

"But how is it possible for anyone to be so foolish as to put papers of any value in the waste-paper basket, even after tearing them up?" Nisard exclaimed, raising his arms. "How is it that they are not burnt?"

"How are you to deal with negligence? Do you suppose that in our offices . . . ?"

"Don't go on!"

MAURICE PALÉOLOGUE

60. EQUIPMENT FOR TIBET

WHEN he had set out, Kintup[1] had been issued with the usual secret service agent's equipment. In the pilgrim's prayer wheel, in place of the rolled paper inscribed with the sacred formula "Om Mani Padme Hum", were a prismatic compass and a roll of paper for making notes. In place of the Tibetan rosary of 108 beads was one of 100 beads for counting paces. But in addition to these normal articles of equipment, Kintup and the monk had been given a number of small metal tubes containing written papers and a drill with which to make the holes for fixing the tubes into the logs they were to float down the river.

LIEUTENANT-COLONEL F. M. BAILEY

[1] A Sikkimese agent of the Survey of India who travelled in Tibet in the 1870's.

61. VODKA WITH PEPPER

WHEN M. poured him three fingers from the frosted carafe Bond took a pinch of black pepper and dropped it on the surface of the vodka. The pepper slowly settled to the bottom of the glass leaving a few grains on the surface which Bond dabbed up with the tip of a finger. Then he tossed the cold liquor well to the back of his throat and put his glass, with the dregs of the pepper at the bottom, back on the table.

M. gave him a glance of rather ironical inquiry.

"It's a trick the Russians taught me that time you attached me to the Embassy in Moscow," apologised Bond. "There's often quite a lot of fusel oil on the surface of this stuff—at least there used to be when it was badly distilled. Poisonous. In Russia, where you get a lot of bath-tub liquor, it's an understood thing to sprinkle a little pepper in your glass. It takes the fusel oil to the bottom."

IAN FLEMING

62. DICHLORETHYL SULPHIDE

IT became advisable to discover who the actual people were who foregathered on certain nights in a certain cottage on the West coast of Ireland. A varnish was invented composed mainly of dichlorethyl sulphide—better known as Mustard Gas. This varnish was spread on the gate, and everybody who went in smeared his hand with it. For an hour nothing happened. But at the end of an hour a sore began to spread. Under the best conditions it takes six weeks for that sore to heal; so that identification became more certain and more simple than even fingerprints could make it.

ROGER LANCELYN GREEN [on Major A. E. W. Mason of the Secret Service]

63. BUTTERFLY-HUNTING IN DALMATIA

ONCE I went "butterfly-hunting" in Dalmatia. I went armed with most effective weapons for the purpose, which have served me well in many a similar campaign. I took a sketch-book, in which were numerous pictures—some finished, others only partly done—of butterflies of every degree and rank, from a "Red Admiral" to a "Painted Lady".

Carrying this book and a colour-box, and a butterfly net in my hand, I was above all suspicion to anyone who met me on the lonely mountain side, even in the neighbourhood of the forts.

I was hunting butterflies, and it was always a good introduction with which to go to anyone who was watching me with suspicion. Quite frankly, with my sketch-book in hand, I would ask innocently whether he had seen such-and-such a butterfly in the neighbourhood, as I was anxious to catch one.

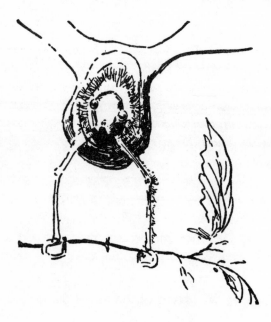

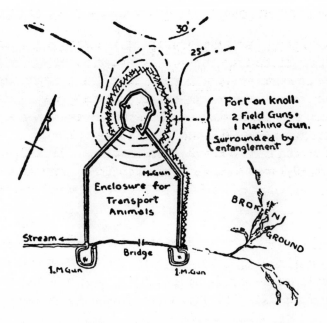

CONCEALING A FORT IN A MOTH'S HEAD

*This sketch was made, giving all the particulars that I wanted.
I then decided to bury it in such a way that it could not be recognised as a fortress plan if I were caught by the military authorities. One idea which occurred to me was to make it into the doorway of a cathedral or church, but I finally decided on the sketch
of the moth's head. Underneath in my note-book I wrote the
following words:*

*"Head of Dula moth as seen through a magnifying glass.
Caught 19.5.12. Magnified about six times the size of life."
(Meaning scale of 6 inches to the mile.)*

This sketch of a butterfly contains the outline of a fortress, and marks both the position and power of the guns. The marks on the wings between *the lines mean nothing, but those* on *the lines show the nature and size of the guns, according to the keys below.*

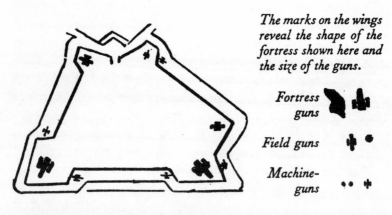

The marks on the wings reveal the shape of the fortress shown here and the size of the guns.

Fortress guns

Field guns

Machine-guns

The position of each gun is at the place inside the outline of the fort on the butterfly where the line marked with the spot ends. The head of the butterfly points towards the north.

Ninety-nine out of a hundred did not know one butterfly from another—any more than I do—so one was on fairly safe ground in that way, and they thoroughly sympathised with the mad Englishman who was hunting these insects.

They did not look sufficiently closely into the sketches of butterflies to notice that the delicately drawn veins of the wings were exact representations, in plan, of their own fort, and that the spots on the wings denoted the number and position of guns and their different calibres.

SIR ROBERT BADEN-POWELL

64. CARRIER PIGEONS

WITH the practical genius of their nation, the English, after long preparation, accomplished a piece of espionage unexampled in the history of the pre-war secret service. They placed agents in the great cities of the Rhine, extending from Holland to Switzerland, and in the German cities on the route Amsterdam–Hanover–Schneidemühl–Thorn. Along this route they flew carrier pigeons, by means of which they could at any time, even in serious emergencies, forward news and information. Early in the year 1914 this organisation was perfected in the most ingenious fashion. The British secret service agents had noted that the carrier pigeons followed, in the one case, the course of the Rhine, and in the other the railway between Amsterdam and Thorn. They now had tiny cameras made, so light that they could be fastened to the birds' tails. These appliances were fitted with clockwork, which at set times would expose portions of a film, and since a whole flight of pigeons was always released simultaneously, and their cameras could be set to make exposures at different times, it would be possible to obtain a fairly continuous series of photographs.

H. R. BERNDORFF

65. A VISIT TO THE LAVATORY

As, holding the lapels of my coat, I tried to review the situation in my mind, I suddenly felt in my breast pocket a notebook, which contained in cryptic form an account of the moneys I had spent. The Cheka agents had ransacked my flat—they were probably searching it at that moment, but they had not thought of searching the clothes we had put on when we were arrested. The notebook was unintelligible to anyone except myself. But it contained figures, and, if it fell into Bolshevik hands, they would find some means of rendering it compromising. They would say that the figures represented movements of Bolshevik troops or moneys I had spent on fomenting counter-revolution. That notebook preyed on my mind. How was I to be rid of it? We might be searched at any moment. In the circumstances there seemed only one solution to the problem. I asked permission of our four sentries to go to the lavatory. It was granted, but the affair was not so simple. Two gunmen accompanied me to the door, but, when I started to close it, they shook their heads. "Leave it open," they said and took up their stand in front of me. It was an embarrassing moment. Should I take the risk or not? Fortunately, the decision was made for me by the insanitary conditions of the place. There was no paper. The walls were smeared with stains of human excrement. As calmly as I could, I took out my notebook, tore out the offending pages and used them in the manner which the circumstances dictated. I pulled the plug. It worked, and I was saved.

R. H. BRUCE LOCKHART

66. TOP PEOPLE READ *THE TIMES*[1]

At half-past twelve o'clock, as Geoffrey Engleheart was busy writing alone in his room at the Foreign Office, he was interrupted by the opening of the door.

"Hulloa, dear boy! I've found my way up here by myself. Busy, as usual, I see!" cried a cheery voice as the door slowly opened, and Geoffrey looking up saw it was his friend Count von Beilstein, well groomed and fashionably attired in glossy silk hat, perfect-fitting frock coat, and varnished boots. He called very frequently upon Engleheart, and had long ago placed himself on excellent terms with the messengers and doorkeepers, who looked upon him as a most generous visitor.

"Oh, how are you?" Engleheart exclaimed, rising and shaking his hand. "You must really forgive me, Count, but I quite forgot my appointment with you today."

"Oh, don't let me disturb you, pray. I'll have a glance at the paper till you've finished," and casting himself into a chair near the window he took up *The Times* and was soon absorbed in it.

A quarter of an hour went by in silence, while Engleheart wrote on, calmly unconscious that there was a small rent in the newspaper the Count was reading, and that through it he could plainly see each word of the treaty as it was transcribed from the secret code and written down in plain English.

"Will you excuse me for ten minutes?" Geoffrey exclaimed presently. "The Cabinet Council is sitting, and I have to run over to see Lord Stanbury for a moment. After I return I must make another copy of this paper, and then I shall be free."

[1] *The Times* is also the only paper ever read by James Bond. See *From Russia with Love* by Ian Fleming.

The Count, casting the newspaper wearily aside, glanced at his watch.

"It's half-past one," he said. "You'll be another half-hour, if not more. After all, I really think, old fellow, I'll go on down to Hurlingham. I arranged to meet the Vaynes at two o'clock."

"All right. I'll run down in a cab as soon as I can get away," answered Engleheart.

"Good. Come on as soon as you can. Violet will be expecting you, you know."

"Of course I shall," replied his unsuspicious friend, and they shook hands, after which the Count put on his hat and sauntered jauntily out.

In Parliament Street he jumped into his phaeton, but instead of driving to Hurlingham gave his man orders to proceed with all speed to the General Post Office, St Martin's-le-Grand. Within half an hour from the time he had shaken the hand of his unsuspecting friend, a message in code—to all intents and purposes a commercial dispatch—was on its way to "Herr Brandt, 116 Friedrich Strasse, Berlin".

That message contained an exact transcript of the secret treaty!

WILLIAM LE QUEUX

67. THE AMBASSADOR'S VALET

JANUARY 6th, 1895. Sandherr's agents are capable of the craziest schemes, the most dangerous acts of temerity. . . . In this connection there is a formidable precedent that could be quoted. If I am not mistaken, it was in 1891—you remember how bad our relations with Britain were at that time, because of Siam. To gain information, Sandherr took into

Count von Beilstein was a spy!

his pay the valet of the Ambassador, Lord Lytton. You also remember that Lytton was a neurotic, who sometimes took champagne to keep himself going and sometimes took drugs to enable him to sleep. In either case he slept very soundly. Every night before going to bed he put the letters and telegrams of the day in a drawer, the key of which, a small golden key strung on a curb-chain, never left him. He used carefully to put it on his night table, with his watch-chain. As soon as he was asleep the valet would creep into his room, take the key, open the drawer, and remove the papers. Then he quickly took them to a house in the Rue d'Aguesseau, where an officer of the intelligence department, Captain Rollin, would be waiting for him. An hour later the papers and golden key would be back in their places. But you can imagine the manner in which the British Government would have demanded redress if it had discovered this violation of human rights, carried out at night, and in the Ambassador's own bedroom, and with the connivance of a serving officer into the bargain. In fact Lord Lytton must have ended by noticing something, because one day he suddenly gave his valet the sack, without giving him any explanation. . . .

MAURICE PALÉOLOGUE

68. RUSSIAN METHODS

IN case the spy, who of course was to move about behind the front as a civilian, were to meet a body of troops accompanied by an officer, he was to act in a particular manner. He was instructed that in such a dangerous predicament he was to squat innocently in the nearest ditch and let down his trousers, as though performing a physical necessity. It is extraordinarily difficult to cross-examine a man in such a position. . . .

Before his departure from enemy territory the spy was to acquire a dog; if necessary he must buy one. This dog was to accompany him on his return. The spy was provided with very thin paper and a small aluminium tube. The paper he covered with his sketches and statistics; he rolled it up and slipped it into the tube, and the tube was inserted in the dog's rectum. There, for a time, no one thought of looking for it. The trick was detected only through a grotesque accident.

A sentry on a country road saw a pedlar trudging along the road with his dog. The dog ran to the edge of the ditch, whining piteously, and apparently anxious to relieve itself. The pedlar, however, would not let him stop, but dragged him along by his leash. The sentry, who was a great lover of animals, felt angry; he ordered the pedlar to let the dog do what it wanted. The poor animal, which was evidently in difficulties, finally got rid of a silvery metal tube. Since the sentry had never heard that dogs were accustomed to excrete such articles, he was struck with amazement, and being an intelligent man he took pedlar, dog and aluminium tube to the guard, and there related the incident. From that time onwards all the military police of this sector examined such dogs as were led about in the neighbourhood of the front by persons in civilian dress.

H. R. BERNDORFF

69. THE EXPLOSIVE CIGAR

SUDDENLY, while the Privy-Councillor lay back in his chair pulling thoughtfully at his cigar, there was a bright, blood-red flash, a dull report, and a man's short agonised cry. Startled, I leaned around the corner of the deck-house, when, to my abject horror, I saw under the electric rays the Czar's Privy-

Councillor lying sideways in his chair with part of his face blown away. Then the hideous truth in an instant became apparent. The cigar which Oberg had pressed upon him down in the saloon had exploded, and the small missile concealed inside the diabolical contrivance had passed upwards into his brain.

WILLIAM LE QUEUX

70. A PLANT

By May [1915] the general outlook which faced the Coalition Government, recently formed by Mr Asquith, was one of much anxiety. Our war plan had broken down, nor was there any hopeful prospect of regaining the initiative. It was the moment to do everything possible to relieve the pressure on the armies in France.

Hall had for some time exploited the obvious method of conveying false information to the Germans by briefing members of his staff to let slip hints about the movements of our ships and troops and forthcoming operations when in company with foreigners whose German sympathies might lead them to pass on the information. Ralph Nevill, who was a well-known figure in London society and in London clubs, earned an unenviable reputation for being highly indiscreet, as he gave members of the foreign embassies and legations a lot of news when lunching and dining with them. Hall himself had the singular experience of being reprimanded by a fellow member of his club for giving away secrets to a comparative stranger.

This was all useful, but now more was required, and he had printed, bound, and weighted in the usual way a Secret Emergency War Code. His plan was to convey this book to the Germans, and then from time to time arrange for messages to be transmitted in the code from our wireless stations. The messages would be unintelligible to our own ships and wireless stations, and so pass unnoticed, but they would be read by the Germans.

The story of the conveyance of the book to Germany, which Hall left amongst his papers, reads like sensational fiction:

'But it was more difficult to convey it into the hands of the enemy in such a way that no suspicion of "planting" would enter their heads. Luckily there was one channel with distinct possibilities. For some little time we had been receiving reports from Holland about a particular hotel in Rotterdam. I need not mention its name, but it was one very frequently used by English people, and by consequence German agents were paying it unusual attention. The hall-porter, we knew, was in German pay, and it had been noticed that if anybody arrived at the hotel from England who seemed in any way "official", a blonde lady would almost inevitably take a room there the next day. We knew, too, not a little about the lady—she was married to a Belgian and was afterwards shot by the French—and we had some respect for her abilities. It was just possible that those abilities could be used to our own advantage.

'There remained the choice of a suitable "victim", and here our good luck held. Mr G. L., now a distinguished figure in the City, was exactly the right man for the job. At that time he was private secretary to a Member of Parliament, but for years he had been in the Foreign Office and was therefore well acquainted with all the official ropes. He could carry a dispatch-case in just the right way. He could assume that manner which, rightly or wrongly, is considered by foreigners to be peculiar to the British diplomatic service. Also he was not without the taste for unusual adventure. I asked him if he would care to take on the job and he joyfully accepted the invitation.

'And so it happened that on the afternoon of Saturday, May 22nd, the day when Lord Fisher first absented himself from the Admiralty, there arrived in Rotterdam a British official, armed with a special passport and carrying "important" papers for the Consulate in an obviously official dispatch-case which also contained a copy of the "new Naval cipher-book". He had deliberately chosen to arrive that particular afternoon, for the Consulate would be closed at any rate until Monday morning and possibly even until Tuesday, for Whit Monday would be intervening, and a British holiday is (or should be) a British holiday wherever you happen to be. There would therefore be nothing for him to do but "hang about" for at least a day and a half, and that was exactly what he desired to do.

'He engaged his room at the hotel, and strolled out into the garden. A well-built hotel, he saw: and the third window from the left on the second floor must surely belong to the room they had given him. The quay, too, was quite close: he might as well have a look at it. And the quay proved interesting, in particular a little piece of it which was crowded with barrels. There was nothing unusual about the barrels themselves, but he walked about amongst them until he had discovered a position from which, while completely hidden himself, he could keep in view the third window from the left on the second floor of his hotel. After which discovery he returned to his room and very carelessly unlocked his dispatch-case before "hiding" it beneath a suit of clothes.

'Nothing unusual happened that evening, but on the Sunday afternoon a lady arrived and asked for a room. She was a blonde lady who seemed to be by herself. She took no notice of the Englishman who was quietly reading in the foyer, and he did not seem to be particularly interested in her.

After dinner, too, he continued to read, and the hall-porter taking pity on a foreigner without friends good-humouredly entered into conversation with him. It must be very dull, he was afraid, for the visitor.

'The visitor agreed, but—what was a man to do on a Sunday?

'The hall-porter smiled, and edged nearer. Perhaps the gentleman would like a little fun?

'The gentleman thought that he would. Unfortunately, he said, he was a stranger to Rotterdam.

'The hall-porter became confidential. There was an exceedingly amusing place to go to in the town. Any gentleman from the hotel would be cordially welcomed. If he cared to be given the address and instructions how to get there . . .

'Five minutes later a very grateful gentleman was hurrying from the hotel. He was so eager, it seemed, for the promised entertainment that he forgot to lock up his dispatch-case. Yet in spite of the careful instructions he never discovered that "amusing place". Once out of sight of the hotel, indeed, he doubled down a side turning, came out on to the quay and hid himself amongst the barrels—with the prospect of a very long wait.

'(Incidentally, it is interesting to note that although the Germans went to some little pains to get L. out of the hotel for some hours, they made no attempt to discover whether he had actually gone downtown. But often enough we would find a blind spot of this kind in their Intelligence work.)

'The blonde lady and her friends wasted little time. Less than half an hour after he had left the hotel, the watcher among the barrels saw the lights switched on in his room. Shadows moved across the blind. Good: they were paying him a visit, and it ought not to take them very long to find the cipher-book. Ah! they must have found it. The light was out. An excellent piece of work. An enemy cipher-book well and truly stolen, almost under its guardian's nose!

'But—what would they do with it? There were some agents who, no doubt, would be content to get away with the spoil; but would the blonde lady be so dreadfully clumsy? No, surely she would favour a subtler plan. She would calculate that the "amusing place" would keep the silly Englishman entertained for at least three hours—more than sufficient time in which to photograph the book page by page and restore it to its hiding-place beneath the clothes. And in that case he would have to remain where he was until the lights in his room had been switched on, and off, again.

'So he waited, and at about 1 a.m. his patience was rewarded. The lights went on for a minute or two. Splendid! The cipher-book had been restored. In a little while it would be safe to return.

'And at half-past one a very "drunken" Englishman reeled into the hotel. He tried to explain to the hall-porter what a good time he had had, but found some difficulty with his words. He also found some difficulty in walking upstairs. The kindly porter put him to bed, and everybody was satisfied.

'I have only to add that about a year later G.L. was sent over to Rotterdam again. The time had come, we judged, when an appendix to the Secret Emergency War Code was about due. This time, however, it was felt that we ought not to give away our most secret ciphers for nothing, and after a little bargaining we were able to sell this appendix to the Germans for £500, which seemed to me to be a fairly good price.'

G.L. is now Sir Guy Locock, who after twelve years at the Foreign Office served on many Government Committees. He was Industrial Adviser in connection with the World Economic Conference, 1933; Member of the Ministry of

Supply Mission to India, 1940–1; Director of the Federation
of British Industries, 1932–45, and Vice-President, 1946.

ADMIRAL SIR WILLIAM JAMES

71. THE GERMAN GOVERNESS

Scene: Private sitting-room of the Wave Crest Hotel, on
the South Coast. September, 1914. It is about 4.30 in the
afternoon. The curtain rises on an empty stage. MRS SANDER-
SON enters and is about to ring the bell, when FRAULEIN
SCHROEDER, returned from a walk, appears upon the verandah.
She peers through the window to ascertain if the room is
occupied, and, having satisfied herself that MRS SANDERSON is
alone, taps upon the panes.

MRS SANDERSON opens the windows to admit her.

Mrs Sanderson: Back already, Luise? You've been very quick.

Fraulein (*moving down to the table and sitting* R. *of it*): I have been
  fortunate. The cliffs were deserted. Everybody was at tea.
  No one to interrupt. But one half-hour, and my drawings
  were complete.

Mrs Sanderson (*as she closes the windows and comes down* R.
  of Fraulein): The harbour defences?

Fraulein: Every detail.

Mrs Sanderson: I congratulate you.

Fraulein: Dank dir, meine Kamaradin.

Mrs Sanderson: Sh! We must still be careful.

              (FRAULEIN SCHROEDER *shrugs her shoulders.*)

Fraulein: The English have no ears. How, then, should their
  walls have them? . . . Where is everybody?

Mrs Sanderson: Need you inquire?

Fraulein (*amused and contemptuous*): At their tea?

Mrs Sanderson: At their tea. Had you brought news that our

Admiral had landed upon their shores, they would still ask for a second cup before inquiring the place of his landing! ... They are a strange people—these enemies of ours!

Fraulein (*with fanatical vehemence*): They are fools and the sons of fools! They dwell in a fool's paradise, and bitter shall be their awakening, for it is into our hands that the Lord has delivered them.

*

THE SIMPLEST THING IN THE WORLD

Brent (*mysteriously*): Ah! That's where "Uzz" comes in!

Miriam (*mystified*): Uzz?

Brent: Yes; don't you remember: "Uzz awaits signal"—what that chap said on the wireless this morning?—Well, I've discovered who "Uzz" is.

Miriam: You have?

Brent: Or rather what it is.

Miriam: It?

Brent: Yes, he's an it!

Miriam: Oh, do explain!

(BRENT *rises, and sits beside her on the Chesterfield.*)

Brent: Well, it's taken me the dickens of a time to worry it out, and it's the simplest thing in the world. In nearly all codes, as we both ought to have remembered, the same sign stands both for letters and for numbers. For instance, A might be one, B two, C three, and so on. Sometimes they work it in a similar way from the opposite end of the alphabet, and in this case I think Z stands for one.

*

AN EARLY MICROPHONE

Miriam: What ever have you got there? A box of cigarettes?

Brent: Looks like it, doesn't it?

Miriam: Then it isn't?

Brent: No, not exactly.

(He opens the lid of the box. It would appear to contain only cigarettes. In point of fact a number of dummy cigarettes have been glued to a stout piece of cardboard, which is secured to the box by hinges, and forms a second and inner lid. Having displayed the cigarettes to MIRIAM, *and to the audience,* BRENT *lifts this lid and discloses a coil of wire to either end of which is attached a disc rather after the style of the receivers employed by telephone operators.)*

*(*MIRIAM *peers into the box.)*

Miriam: It isn't dangerous, is it?

Brent (laughing): Not to you! As a matter of fact, it's rather a cute little dodge—generally known as "The Eavesdropper's Friend"!

(He gives the box to MIRIAM, *and walks upstage* R., *uncoiling the wires from it as he goes.)*

It'll detect sounds entirely indistinguishable by the naked ear, and convey them quite clearly for a mile or more. Oh, it's a useful little feller!

(Whilst he has been talking he has been busily engaged in concealing one end of the apparatus amongst the foliage of a palm near by the window. With MIRIAM'S *assistance he slips the remainder of the coil through the space between the window-doors and the floor. Then he goes out by the window for a moment, conceals the receiver on the verandah, and returns.)*

There! "Little boys should be seen and not heard." Well, if necessary, this little boy's going to hear and not be seen! Comes to the same thing, doesn't it?

(He closes the window. MIRIAM *laughs and moves* C. *above the table.)*

Miriam: Oh, Kit, you're a wonderful person! Every time I see you you've got some new trick.

LECHMERE WORRALL and J. E. HAROLD TERRY

72. THE HANSOM CAB APPROACH

AT a rather late hour that night the Confidential Secretary put the minutes of the meeting together with the map-tracing and notes into a lock-up portfolio and took a hansom from Arlington Street to Downing Street with the object of putting the contents of the portfolio in safety among the other State papers in the keeping of the Foreign Office.

It was a dark, miserable, drizzly night, and when the driver asked him if he should let the glass down he said, "Yes." While they were going through an almost deserted square the man raised the trap-door gently and passed the end of a thin india-rubber tube into the cab. Then he pressed the bulb of a large spray producer concealed under his cape, and when he had continued this for about a couple of minutes he closed the trap down hard.

The Confidential Secretary did not reach Downing Street that night. The next morning soon after daybreak a policeman saw a driverless cab on Wimbledon Common being slowly drawn hither and thither as the horse grazed. Inside the cab were found the dead body of the Secretary and a complete cabman's outfit—clothes, top coat, tarpaulin hat and cape, and even boots. The portfolio with its priceless contents was gone.

GEORGE GRIFFITH

73. CALLOWAY'S CODE

[Described by Bernard Newman in *Secrets of German Espionage* as "a favourite study in espionage circles".]

THE New York *Enterprise* sent H. B. Calloway as special correspondent to the Russo-Japanese-Portsmouth war.

For two months Calloway hung about Yokohama and Tokio, shaking dice with the other correspondents for drinks of "rickshaws"—oh, no, that's something to ride in; anyhow, he wasn't earning the salary that his paper was paying him. But that was not Calloway's fault. The little brown men who held the strings of Fate between their fingers were not ready for the readers of the *Enterprise* to season their breakfast bacon and eggs with the battles of the descendants of the gods.

But soon the column of correspondents that were to go out with the First Army tightened their field-glass belts and went down to the Yalu with Kuroki. Calloway was one of these.

Now, this is no history of the battle of the Yalu River. That has been told in detail by the correspondents who gazed at the shrapnel smoke-rings from a distance of three miles. But, for justice's sake, let it be understood that the Japanese commander prohibited a nearer view.

Calloway's feat was accomplished before the battle. What he did was to furnish the *Enterprise* with the biggest beat of the war. That paper published exclusively and in detail the news of the attack on the lines of the Russian General Zassulitch on the same day that it was made. No other paper printed a word about it for two days afterwards, except a London paper, whose account was absolutely incorrect and untrue.

Calloway did this in face of the fact that General Kuroki was making his moves and laying his plans with the profoundest secrecy as far as the world outside his camps was concerned. The correspondents were forbidden to send out any news whatever of his plans; and every message that was allowed on the wires was censored with rigid severity.

The correspondent for the London paper handed in a cablegram describing Kuroki's plans; but as it was wrong from beginning to end the censor grinned and let it go through.

So, there they were—Kuroki on one side on the Yalu with forty-two thousand infantry, five thousand cavalry, and one hundred and twenty-four guns. On the other side, Zassulitch waited for him with only twenty-three thousand men, and with a long stretch of river to guard. And Calloway had got hold of some important inside information that he knew would bring the *Enterprise* staff around a cablegram as thick as flies around a Park Row lemonade stand. If he could only get that message past the censor—the new censor who had arrived and taken his post that day.

Calloway did the obviously proper thing. He lit his pipe and sat down on a gun carriage to think it over. And there we must leave him; for the rest of the story belongs to Vesey, a sixteen-dollar-a-week reporter on the *Enterprise*.

Calloway's cablegram was handed to the managing editor at four o'clock in the afternoon. He read it three times; and then drew a pocket mirror from a pigeon-hole in his desk, and looked at his reflection carefully. Then he went over to the desk of Boyd, his assistant (he usually called Boyd when he wanted him), and laid the cablegram before him.

"It's from Calloway," he said. "See what you make of it."

The message was dated at Wi-ju, and these were the words of it:

> Foregone preconcerted rash witching goes muffled rumour mine dark silent unfortunate richmond existing great hotly brute select mooted parlous beggars ye angel incontrovertible.

Boyd read it twice.

"It's either a cipher or a sunstroke," said he.

"Ever hear of anything like a code in the office—a secret code?" asked the m.e., who had held his desk for only two years. Managing editors come and go.

"None except the vernacular that the lady specials write in," said Boyd. "Couldn't be an acrostic, could it?"

"I thought of that," said the m.e., "but the beginning letters contain only four vowels. It must be a code of some sort."

"Try 'em in groups," suggested Boyd. "Let's see—'Rash witching goes'—not with me it doesn't. 'Muffled rumour mine'—must have an underground wire. 'Dark silent unfortunate richmond'—no reason why he should knock that town so hard. 'Existing great hotly'—no, it doesn't pan out. I'll call Scott."

The city editor came in a hurry, and tried his luck. A city editor must know something about everything, so Scott knew a little about cipher-writing.

"It may be what is called an inverted alphabet cipher," said he. "I'll try that. 'R' seems to be the oftenest used initial letter, with the exception of 'm'. Assuming 'r' to mean 'e', the most frequently used vowel, we transpose the letters—so."

Scott worked rapidly with his pencil for two minutes; and then showed the first word according to his reading—the word "Scejtzez".

"Great!" cried Boyd. "It's a charade. My first is a Russian general. Go on, Scott."

"No, that won't work," said the city editor. "It's undoubtedly a code. It's impossible to read it without the key. Has the office ever used a cipher code?"

"Just what I was asking," said the m.e. "Hustle everybody up that ought to know. We must get at it some way. Calloway has evidently got hold of something big, and the censor has put the screws on, or he wouldn't have cabled in a lot of chop-suey like this."

Throughout the office of the *Enterprise* a drag-net was sent, hauling in such members of the staff as would be likely to know of a code, past or present, by reason of their wisdom, information, natural intelligence, or length of servitude. They got together in a group in the city room, with the m.e. in the centre. No one had heard of a code. All began to explain to the head investigator that newspapers never use a code, anyhow—that is, a cipher code. Of course the Associated Press stuff is a sort of code—an abbreviation, rather—but——

The m.e. knew all that, and said so. He asked each man how long he had worked on the paper. Not one of them had drawn pay from an *Enterprise* envelope for longer than six years.

Calloway had been on the paper twelve years.

"Try old Heffelbauer," said the m.e. "He was here when Park Row was a potato patch."

Heffelbauer was an institution. He was half janitor, half handyman about the office, and half watchman—thus becoming the peer of thirteen and one-half tailors. Sent for, he came, radiating his nationality.

"Heffelbauer," said the m.e., "did you ever hear of a code belonging to the office a long time ago—a private code? You know what a code is, don't you?"

"Yah," said Heffelbauer. "Sure I know vat a code is. Yah, apout dwelf or fifteen year ago der office had a code. Der reborters in der city room haf it here."

"Ah!" said the m.e. "We're getting on the trail now. Where was it kept, Heffelbauer? What do you know about it?"

"Somedimes," said the retainer, "dey deep it in der little room behind der library room."

"Can you find it?" asked the m.e. eagerly. "Do you know where it is?"

"Mein Gott!" said Heffelbauer. "How long you dink a code live? Der reborters call him a masket. But von day he butt mit head der editor, und——"

"Oh, he's talking about a goat," said Boyd. "Get out, Heffelbauer."

Again discomfited, the concerted wit and resource of the *Enterprise* huddled around Calloway's puzzle, considering its mysterious words in vain.

Then Vesey came in.

Vesey was the youngest reporter. He had a thirty-two-inch chest and wore a number fourteen collar; but his bright Scotch plaid suit gave him presence and conferred no obscurity upon his whereabouts. He wore his hat in such a position that people followed him about to see him take it off, convinced that it must be hung upon a peg driven into the back of his head. He was never without an immense, knotted, hard-wood cane with a German-silver tip on its crooked handle. Vesey was the best photograph hustler in the office. Scott said it was because no living human being could resist the personal triumph it was to hand his picture over to Vesey. Vesey always wrote his own news stories, except the big ones, which were sent to the rewrite man. Add to this fact that among all the inhabitants, temples, and groves of the earth nothing existed that could abash Vesey, and his dim sketch is concluded.

Vesey butted into the circle of cipher readers very much as Heffelbauer's "code" would have done, and asked what was up. Someone explained, with the touch of half-familiar condescension that they always used towards him. Vesey reached out and took the cablegram from the m.e.'s hand. Under the protection of some special Providence, he was always doing appalling things like that, and coming off unscathed.

"It's a code," said Vesey. "Anybody got the key?"

"The office has no code," said Boyd, reaching for the message. Vesey held to it.

"Then old Calloway expects us to read it, anyhow," said

he. "He's up a tree, or something, and he's made this up so as to get it by the censor. It's up to us. Gee! I wish they had sent me too. Say—we can't afford to fall down on our end of it. 'Foregone, preconcerted rash, witching' —h'm."

Vesey sat down on a table corner and began to whistle softly, frowning at the cablegram.

"Let's have it, please," said the m.e. "We've got to get to work on it."

"I believe I've got a line on it," said Vesey. "Give me ten minutes."

He walked to his desk, threw his hat into a waste-basket, spread out flat on his chest like a gorgeous lizard, and started his pencil going. The wit and wisdom of the *Enterprise* remained in a loose group, and smiled at one another, nodding their heads towards Vesey. Then they began to exchange their theories about the cipher.

It took Vesey exactly fifteen minutes. He brought to the m.e. a pad with the code-key written on it.

"I felt the swing of it as soon as I saw it," said Vesey. "Hurrah for old Calloway! He's done the Japs and every paper in town that prints literature instead of news. Take a look at that."

Thus had Vesey set forth the reading of the code:

> Foregone—conclusion
> Preconcerted—arrangement
> Rash—act
> Witching—hour of midnight
> Goes—without saying
> Muffled—report
> Rumour—hath it
> Mine—host
> Dark—horse
> Silent—majority

Unfortunate—pedestrians[1]
Richmond—in the field
Existing—conditions
Great—White Way
Hotly—contested
Brute—force
Select—few
Mooted—question
Parlous—times
Beggars—description
Ye—correspondent
Angel—unawares
Incontrovertible—fact

"It's simply newspaper English," explained Vesey. "I've been reporting on the *Enterprise* long enough to know it by heart. Old Calloway gives us the cue word, and we use the word that naturally follows it just as we use 'em in the paper. Read it over, and you'll see how pat they drop into their places. Now, here's the message he intended us to get."

Vesey handed out another sheet of paper.

Concluded arrangement to act at hour of midnight without saying. Report hath it that a large body of cavalry and an overwhelming force of infantry will be thrown into the field. Conditions white. Way contested by only a small force. Question the *Times* description. Its correspondent is unaware of the facts.

"Great stuff!" cried Boyd excitedly. "Kuroki crosses the Yalu tonight and attacks. Oh, we won't do a thing to the sheets that make up with Addison's essays, real estate transfers, and bowling scores!"

[1] Mr Vesey afterwards explained that the logical journalistic complement of the word "unfortunate" was once the word "victim". But since the automobile became so popular, the correct following word was now "pedestrians". Of course, in Calloway's code it meant infantry.

"Mr Vesey," said the m.e., with his jollying-which-you-should-regard-as-a-favour manner, "you have cast a serious reflection upon the literary standards of the paper that employs you. You have also assisted materially in giving us the biggest 'beat' of the year. I will let you know in a day or two whether you are to be discharged or retained at a larger salary. Somebody send Ames to me."

Ames was the king-pin, the snowy-petalled marguerite, the star-bright looloo of the rewrite men. He saw attempted murder in the pains of green-apple colic, cyclones in the summer zephyr, lost children in every top-spinning urchin, an uprising of the down-trodden masses in every hurling of a derelict potato at a passing automobile. When not rewriting, Ames sat on the porch of his Brooklyn villa playing checkers with his ten-year-old son.

Ames and the "war-editor" shut themselves in a room. There was a map in there stuck full of little pins that represented armies and divisions. Their fingers had been itching for days to move those pins along the crooked line of the Yalu. They did so now; and in words of fire Ames translated Calloway's brief message into a front-page masterpiece that set the world talking. He told of the secret councils of the Japanese officers; gave Kuroki's flaming speeches in full; counted the cavalry and infantry to a man and a horse; described the quick and silent building of the bridge at Suikauchen, across which the Mikado's legions were hurled upon the surprised Zassulitch, whose troops were widely scattered along the river. And the battle!—well, you know what Ames can do with a battle if you give him just one smell of smoke for a foundation. And in the same story, with seemingly supernatural knowledge, he gleefully scored the most profound and ponderous paper in England for the false and misleading account of the Japanese First Army printed in its issue of *the same date*.

Only one error was made; and that was the fault of the cable operator at Wi-ju. Calloway pointed it out after he came back. The word "great" in his code should have been "gauge", and its complemental words "of battle". But it went to Ames "conditions white", and of course he took that to mean snow. His description of the Japanese army struggling through the snowstorm, blinded by the whirling flakes, was thrillingly vivid. The artists turned out some effective illustrations that made a hit as pictures of the artillery dragging their guns through the drifts. But, as the attack was made on the first day of May, the "conditions white" excited some amusement. But it made no difference to the *Enterprise*, anyway.

It was wonderful. And Calloway was wonderful in having made the new censor believe that his jargon of words meant no more than a complaint of the dearth of news and a petition for more expense money. And Vesey was wonderful. And most wonderful of all are words, and how they make friends one with another, being oft associated until not even obituary notices them do part.

On the second day following, the city editor halted at Vesey's desk where the reporter was writing the story of a man who had broken his leg by falling into a coal-hole— Ames having failed to find a murder motive in it.

"The old man says your salary is to be raised to twenty a week," said Scott.

"All right," said Vesey. "Every little helps. Say—Mr Scott, which would you say—'We can state without fear of successful contradiction', or 'On the whole it can be safely asserted'?"

O. HENRY

Epilogue

WHILE we were collecting material for this book I went one day to a second-hand bookshop in London which specialises in old detective stories and thrillers. I asked the girl in the shop if they had any spy stories in stock. A look of suspicion came over her face. "What foreign government do you represent?" she asked.

I told her that I only represented myself and with some difficulty extracted from her the story behind her question.

They had had an order from the agent of a foreign government for any book they could provide, fact or fiction, which so much as mentioned a spy. The result had been between forty and fifty large parcels, which brought them in about £150 and completely cleared out their stock of spy books.

"I hope," I said, "that they are enjoying the books in Moscow."

"It wasn't the Russians," she replied. "It was the Germans."

Remembering an incident in the Cicero case, I said I hoped the Germans would get some good ideas. For instance, they might consider the formation of a Waiters' Underground as described in E. Phillips Oppenheim's *The Secret*. "That," she said rather unhappily, "was one of the books we sold them."

So now, one can believe, parcels of William Le Queux, E. Phillips Oppenheim and many other authors represented in these pages are being opened by puzzled German Embassy secretaries and other less official agents all over the world. L. C. Moyzisch in *Operation Cicero* describes how one day soon after he had made Cicero's acquaintance he received by carrier post from Berlin a somewhat surprising present.

"It was a huge parcel which, when opened, turned out to be an almost complete collection of books dealing with the more celebrated cases of espionage in the twentieth century. There were various White Papers and official files, together with quite a few works of fiction. I had not ordered these books and had neither the time nor the desire to read them. There was a covering note, in which I was more or less tactfully informed that a thorough study of these books would help me in handling Operation Cicero. I shoved them all firmly into the back of the bottom drawer of my desk and there they remained, an unread monument to German thoroughness."

No doubt such parcels in the future will always include at least one copy of *The Spy's Bedside Book*.

HUGH GREENE

To: Carroll & Graf Publishers, Inc.
        260 Fifth Avenue
        New York, New York 10001

..................................Embassy *
..................................Legation *
......................Consulate-General *

I should like to take advantage of your offer to supply to
any authorised agent of a foreign government copies of
The Spy's Bedside Book at the ordinary trade discount.
I guarantee that these copies will not be sold at any
bookshop, drugstore, library or other commercial
establishment, but will be used only for the proper
purposes of our Secret Services.

I require...............copies. (*Postage free on any order
over 100.*)

        Signed....................................

                        1st Secretary *
                    Military Attaché *
                    Naval Attaché *
                        Air Attaché *
                    Consul-General *

    * Please delete where inapplicable.

Bibliography

1. John Buchan: *Greenmantle* (Hodder and Stoughton, 1916)
2. *Report of the Royal Commission to investigate the facts relating to and the circumstances surrounding the communication, by public officials and other persons in positions of trust, of secret and confidential information to agents of a foreign power. June 27, 1946* (Ottawa, Edmond Cloutier, C.M.G., B.A., L.Ph., Printer to the King's Most Excellent Majesty, Controller of Stationery, 1946)
3. W. Somerset Maugham: *Ashenden* (Heinemann, 1928)
4. L. C. Moyzisch: *Operation Cicero* (Allan Wingate, 1950)
5. Sir Robert Baden-Powell: *My Adventures as a Spy* (C. Arthur Pearson, 1915)
6. Bernard Newman: *Secrets of German Espionage* (Robert Hale, 1940)
7. William Le Queux: *The Hunchback of Westminster* (Methuen, 1904)
8. T. E. Lawrence: *Seven Pillars of Wisdom* (Jonathan Cape, 1926)
9. William Le Queux: *Secrets of the Foreign Office* (Hutchinson, 1903)
10. Herbert Greene: *Secret Agent in Spain* (Robert Hale, 1938)
11. Dennis Wheatley: *Mediterranean Nights* (Hutchinson, 1942)
12. William Le Queux: *Revelations of the Secret Service* (F. V. White, 1911)
13. Vladimir and Evdokia Petrov: *Empire of Fear* (André Deutsch, 1956)

14. Peter Fleming: *Invasion 1940* (Rupert Hart-Davis, 1957)

15. George Griffith: *The Outlaws of the Air* (Tower Publishing Company, 1895)

16. Fenimore Cooper: *The Spy* (G. and W. B. Whitaker, 1822)

17. W. H. Auden: *Poems* (Faber and Faber, 1930)

18. See 9 above

19. Graham Greene: *The Basement Room* (Cresset Press, 1935)

20. See 14 above

21. Anna Seward: "Monody on Major André", *Poetical Works*, edited by Walter Scott (James Ballantyne and Company, Edinburgh, 1810)
The Dictionary of National Biography, Volume 1 (Clarendon Press)

22. Joseph Conrad: *Under Western Eyes* (Methuen, 1911)

23. Max Pemberton: *Pro Patria* (Ward, Lock, 1901)

24. See 12 above

25. Sir Paul Dukes: *The Story of ST. 25* (Cassell, 1949)

26. Belle Boyd: *Belle Boyd in Camp and Prison* (Saunders Otley, 1865)

27. Maurice Paléologue: *My Secret Diary of the Dreyfus Case* (Secker and Warburg, 1957)

28. Ian Fleming: *From Russia with Love* (Jonathan Cape, 1957)
The Schellenberg Memoirs (André Deutsch, 1956)

29. Lechmere Worrall and J. E. Harold Terry: *The Man Who Stayed at Home* (Samuel French, 1916)

30. Arthur Morrison: *Martin Hewitt, Investigator* (Ward, Lock and Bowden, 1894)

31. Compton Mackenzie: *Greek Memories* (Chatto and Windus, 1939)

32. Colette: *My Apprenticeships* (Secker and Warburg, 1957)

33. Edmund Blunden: *Undertones of War* (Cobden Sanderson, 1928)
34. See 9 above
35. Rudyard Kipling: *The Years Between* (Methuen, 1919)
36. Alan H. Burgoyne: *The War Inevitable* (Francis Griffiths, 1908)
37. Richard Harding Davis: *Once Upon a Time* (Duckworth, 1911)
38. Robert Browning: *Men and Women* (1855)
39. See 5 above
40. See 9 above
41. E. Phillips Oppenheim: *The Secret* (Ward, Lock, 1907)
42. See 9 above
43. See 28 above
44. Ian Fleming: *Casino Royale* (Jonathan Cape, 1953)
45. See 16 above
46. R. H. Bruce Lockhart: *Memoirs of a British Agent* (Putnam, 1932)
47. Eric Ambler: *The Mask of Dimitrios* (Hodder and Stoughton, 1939)
48. See 21 above
49. Sir Basil Thomson: *Queer People* (Hodder and Stoughton, 1922)
50. Hugh Kingsmill: *D. H. Lawrence* (Methuen, 1938)
51. Thomas Mann: *Joseph and His Brothers* (Secker and Warburg, 1956)
52. William Blake: *Letters*, edited by Geoffrey Keynes (Rupert Hart-Davis, 1956)
    William Blake: *The Writings of William Blake*, edited by Geoffrey Keynes (Nonesuch Press, 1925)
53. Samuel Taylor Coleridge: *Biographia Literaria* (1817)
    Mary Moorman: *William Wordsworth* (Oxford University Press, 1957)
54. *Intimate Journals of Paul Gauguin* (Jonathan Cape, 1923)

55. *Documents on German Foreign Policy, 1918–1945*. Series D, Volume X. The War Years 23 June–31 August 1940 (H.M. Stationery Office, 1957)

56. See 27 above

57. Guy Chapman: *The Dreyfus Case* (Rupert Hart-Davis, 1955)

58. Thomas Hardy: *The Dynasts* (Macmillan, 1910)

59. See 27 above

60. Lt.-Col. F. M. Bailey: *No Passport to Tibet* (Rupert Hart-Davis, 1957)

61. Ian Fleming: *Moonraker* (Jonathan Cape, 1955)

62. Roger Lancelyn Green: *A. E. W. Mason* (Max Parrish, 1952)

63. See 5 above

64. H. R. Berndorff: *Espionage* (Nash and Grayson, 1930)

65. See 46 above

66. William Le Queux: *The Great War in England 1897* (Tower Publishing Company, 1894)

67. See 27 above

68. See 64 above

69. William Le Queux: *The Czar's Spy* (Hodder and Stoughton, 1905)

70. Admiral Sir William James: *The Eyes of the Navy* (Methuen, 1955)

71. See 29 above

72. George Griffith: *The Great Pirate Syndicate* (F. V. White, 1899)

73. O. Henry: *Whirligigs* (Hodder and Stoughton, 1916)

The frontispiece and the illustration on page 92 are taken from William Le Queux: *Spies of the Kaiser* (Hurst and Blackett, 1909)